CIPS Study Matters

Level 3

Certificate in Purchasing and Supply

WITHDRAWN FROM
ST HELENS COLLEGE LIBRARY

Purchasing Operations

Stephen Kirby
Independent Procurement Consultant

THE
CHARTERED INSTITUTE OF
PURCHASING & SUPPLY

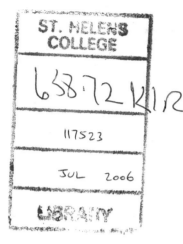

ST. HELENS
COLLEGE

658.72 KIR

117523

JUL 2006

LIBRARY

Published by

The Chartered Institute of Purchasing and Supply
Easton House, Easton on the Hill, Stamford, Lincolnshire PE9 3NZ
Tel: +44 (0) 1780 756 777
Fax: +44 (0) 1780 751 610
Email: info@cips.org
Website: http://www.cips.org

© The Chartered Institute of Purchasing and Supply 2006

First published June 2006

All rights reserved. No part of this publication may be reproduced, stored in
a retrieval system, or transmitted, in any form or by any means, electronic,
mechanical, photocopying, recording or otherwise without permission of
the copyright owner.

While every effort has been made to ensure that references to websites
are correct at time of going to press, the world wide web is a constantly
changing environment and CIPS cannot accept any responsibility for any
changes to addresses.

CIPS acknowledges product, service and company names referred to in this
publication, many of which are trade names, service marks, trademarks or
registered trademarks.

CIPS, The Chartered Institute of Purchasing & Supply and its logo are all
trademarks of the Chartered Institute of Purchasing & Supply.

The right of Stephen Kirby to be identified as author of this work has been
asserted by him in accordance with the Copyright, Designs and Patents
Act, 1988 in force or as amended from time to time.

Technical reviewer: Garry Bradley, GB Associates

Instructional design and publishing project management by Wordhouse
Ltd, Reading, UK

Content management system, instructional editing and pre-press by
Echelon Learning Ltd, London, UK

Index prepared by Indexing Specialists (UK) Ltd, Hove, UK

ISBN 1-86124-149-6
ISBN 978-186124-149-8

Contents

Introduction **vii**

Unit content coverage **xi**

Study session 1: Purchasing objectives in different types of organisation **1**
    The nature of different types of organisation **2**
    Purchasing objectives in a manufacturing company **3**
    Typical purchasing objectives in a service organisation **5**
    Typical purchasing objectives in a retail organisation including
        FMCG **6**
    Purchasing objectives in not-for-profit organisations **8**

Study session 2: Obtaining the right quality **13**
    Quality as either 'conformance to specification' or 'fitness for
        purpose' **14**
    The costs involved in getting quality wrong **15**
    Introduction to the principles of managing supplier quality **17**

Study session 3: Obtaining the right quantity **23**
    How to determine the quantity of goods or materials required,
        including determining demand factors **24**
    Minimum order quantities (MOQ) **25**
    Economic order quantity and how to calculate it **27**
    Stock replenishment systems including the calculation of reorder points
        and buffer (or 'insurance') stocks (also known as 'safety stock') **29**

Study session 4: Ensuring delivery to the right place **35**
    Ensuring that deliveries are made to the right place, why it is important,
        and why it might not happen in practice **36**
    Different transport types and their advantages and disadvantages **37**
    How to select the type(s) of transport to use **40**
    International transport documentation including Incoterms **41**
    Packaging considerations **43**

Study session 5: Ensuring delivery at the right time **47**
    Different types of lead time **48**
    Further lead time considerations **50**
    Expediting to ensure delivery times are met **51**
    Measuring supplier delivery performance **52**
    Logistics operators' systems **52**

Study session 6: Obtaining the right price **57**
    The importance of paying the right price **58**
    Types of cost incurred by suppliers and their impact on price **59**
    Factors that might affect how a supplier prices its products or
        services **61**

Study session 7: The purpose and importance of specifications **67**
    The meaning of specifications and tolerances **68**
    The importance and purpose of developing specifications for
        products **69**

Service specifications **70**
The need for the buyer to 'drive' the specification **72**
The importance of the supplier demonstrating the methodology used in delivering products and services **73**

Study session 8: Different types of specification **77**
Different types of specification in common use **78**
The sectors in which each type of specification is used **81**
Why performance specifications are being used more and more **82**
Standards and their uses **84**

Study session 9: The contribution of buyers and sellers to specifications **89**
The contribution that buyers and suppliers can make to the specification process **90**
Early buyer involvement (EBI) **91**
Early supplier involvement (ESI) **93**

Study session 10: Information requirements for effective specifications **97**
'Bespoke' (made to order) versus 'standard' (readily available) **98**
The technical requirements for different types of purchase: materials, services, and so on **99**
Timescales, costs and budgets for expenditure **100**

Study session 11: Internal and external influences on specifications **107**
Corporate social responsibility, ethics and conflict of interest **108**
Quality standards and 'kite marks' **109**
Pricing and payment practices and their effect on specifications **110**

Study session 12: The purchasing 'cycle' **115**
Identification of needs and specification development **116**
Surveying the market, selecting the most promising supplier and supplier appraisal **117**
Inviting and analysing quotations **119**
Negotiation **120**
Monitoring and reviewing performance **121**

Study session 13: Identification and evaluation of supply sources **125**
Sources of information on potential suppliers **126**
Obtaining information on potential suppliers **127**
Information required about potential suppliers **128**

Study session 14: Documentation requirements for effective sourcing **133**
Capability surveys and approved supplier lists **134**
Requests for quotation **136**
Vendor rating **138**
Documentation in the purchase-to-pay process **138**
Payment methods **140**

Study session 15: Verification of suppliers' capabilities **145**
Following up suppliers' references **146**
Carrying out a financial assessment of a supplier **147**
Specific aspects of supplier performance **152**

Study session 16: The legal system **157**
    Differences between common law and statute law **158**
    Criminal law and civil law and different types of court **159**
    The role of European law in the English legal system **161**

Study session 17: Contract formation **165**
    The nature and significance of 'offer' and 'acceptance' in contract
        formation **166**
    The nature and significance of 'consideration', 'intention to be legally
        bound', 'capacity' and 'legality' in forming contracts **167**
    Templates and standard contractual forms **169**

Study session 18: Contract terms and conditions **173**
    The role of terms and conditions of contract **174**
    Conditions, warranties and express or implied terms **176**
    'Special' contract terms **177**

Study session 19: Privity of contract **183**
    The concept of privity of contract and its effect on contract
        formation **184**
    Exceptions to the 'privity' concept **185**
    The Contracts (Rights of Third Parties) Act 1999 **185**

Study session 20: Contract dispute resolution **189**
    The role and significance of negotiation as a means of dispute
        resolution **190**
    The role and significance of adjudication and arbitration as means of
        dispute resolution **191**
    The role and significance of litigation as a means of dispute
        resolution **192**

Revision questions **195**

Feedback on revision questions **201**

References and bibliography **215**

Index **217**

Introduction

This course book has been designed to assist you in studying for the CIPS Purchasing Operations unit in the Level 3 Certificate in Purchasing and Supply. The book covers all topics in the official CIPS unit content document, as illustrated in the table beginning on page xi.

This book aims to provide an overview of general procurement principles but at all times focusing on practical implications. It is targeted at people who have recently started a procurement role and attempts to provide a sound practical background to everyday purchasing activities of a kind that are likely to be encountered by all personnel working in a purchasing environment.

To this end the book starts by examining different purchasing environments, the intention here being to provide an overview of how purchasing operates in different situations such as manufacturing organisations, service providers and not-for-profit organisations amongst others. It then moves on to examine one of the most basic elements of purchasing – the 'five rights' – the concept of ensuring that all purchases represent the best buy taking account of delivery at the right time, to the right place, paying the right price, receiving the right quality of goods or service and receiving the right quantity. The next aspect of purchasing to be examined is that of specifications. Many purchasing personnel do not regard these as being a 'core' purchasing activity but they provide the basis for ensuring that the 'right' item or service is purchased.

We then move on to examining the purchasing cycle – the sequence of purchasing activities that take place in all organisations irrespective of type, starting with identification of need and moving through such activities as sourcing, negotiation and contract award, before finishing with payment of invoices and vendor rating. There is particular emphasis on general sourcing, including locating potential sources of supply, supplier appraisal and vendor rating. The book ends with a comprehensive overview of the legal implications of purchasing, focusing particularly on contract formation and dispute resolution.

How to use this book

The course book will take you step by step through the unit content in a series of carefully planned 'study sessions' and provides you with learning activities, self-assessment questions and revision questions to help you master the subject matter. The guide should help you organise and carry out your studies in a methodical, logical and effective way, but if you have your own study preferences you will find it a flexible resource too.

Before you begin using course this book, make sure you are familiar with any advice provided by CIPS on such things as study skills, revision techniques or support and how to handle formal assessments.

If you are on a taught course, it will be up to your tutor to explain how to use the book – when to read the study sessions, when to tackle the activities and questions, and so on.

If you are on a self-study course, or studying independently, you can use the course book in the following way:

- Scan the whole book to get a feel for the nature and content of the subject matter.
- Plan your overall study schedule so that you allow enough time to complete all 20 study sessions well before your examinations – in other words, leaving plenty of time for revision.
- For each session, set aside enough time for reading the text, tackling all the learning activities and self-assessment questions, and the revision question at the end of the session, and for the suggested further reading. Guidance on roughly how long you should set aside for studying each session is given at the beginning of the session.

Now let's take a look at the structure and content of the individual study sessions.

Overview of the study sessions

The course book breaks the content down into 20 sessions, which vary from three to six or seven hours' duration each. However, we are not advising you to study for this sort of time without a break! The sessions are simply a convenient way of breaking the syllabus into manageable chunks. Most people would try to study one or two sessions a week, taking one or two breaks within each session. You will quickly find out what suits you best.

Each session begins with a brief **introduction** which sets out the areas of the syllabus being covered and explains, if necessary, how the session fits in with the topics that come before and after.

After the introduction there is a statement of the **session learning objectives**. The objectives are designed to help you understand exactly what you should be able to do after you've studied the session. You might find it helpful to tick them off as you progress through the session. You will also find them useful during revision. There is one session learning objective for each numbered subsection of the session.

After this, there is a brief section reproducing the learning objectives and indicative content from the official **unit content document**. This will help you to understand exactly which part of the syllabus you are studying in the current session.

Following this, there are **prior knowledge** and **resources** sections if necessary. These will let you know if there are any topics you need to be familiar with before tackling each particular session, or any special resources you might need, such as a calculator or graph paper.

Then the main part of the study session begins, with the first of the numbered main subsections. At regular intervals in each study session, we have provided you with **learning activities**, which are designed to get you actively involved in the learning process. You should always try to complete the activities – usually on a separate sheet of your own paper – before reading on. You will learn much more effectively if you are actively involved in doing something as you study, rather than just passively reading the text in front of you. The feedback or answers to the activities are provided at the end of the session. Do not be tempted to skip the activity.

We also provide a number of **self-assessment questions** in each study session. These are to help you to decide for yourself whether or not you have achieved the learning objectives set out at the beginning of the session. As with the activities, you should always tackle them – usually on a separate sheet of paper. Don't be tempted to skip them. The feedback or answers are again at the end of the session. If you still do not understand a topic having attempted the self-assessment question, always try to re-read the relevant passages in the textbook readings or session, or follow the advice on further reading at the end of the session. If this still doesn't work, you should contact the CIPS Membership and Qualification Advice team.

For most of the learning activities and self assessment questions you will need to use separate sheets of paper for your answers or responses. Some of the activities or questions require you to complete a table or form, in which case you could write your response in the study guide itself, or photocopy the page.

At the end of the session are three final sections.

The first is the **summary**. Use it to remind yourself or check off what you have just studied, or later on during revision.

Then follows the **suggested further reading** section. This section, if it appears, contains recommendations for further reading which you can follow up if you would like to read alternative treatments of the topics. If for any reason you are having difficulty understanding the course book on a particular topic, try one of the alternative treatments recommended. If you are keen to read around and beyond the syllabus, to help you pick up extra points in the examination for example, you may like to try some of the additional readings recommended. If this section does not appear at the end of a session, it usually means that further reading for the session topics is not necessary.

At the end of the session we direct you to a **revision question**, which you will find in a separate section at the end of the course book. Feedback on the questions is also given.

Reading lists

CIPS produces an official reading list, which recommends essential and desirable texts for augmenting your studies. This reading list is available on the CIPS website or from the CIPS Bookshop. This course book is one of the essential texts for this unit. In this section we describe the main characteristics of the other essential text for this unit, which you are strongly urged to buy and use throughout your course.

The other essential text is:

Purchasing and Supply Chain Management by K Lysons and B Farrington, 7th edition, published by FT Prentice Hall (2006)

This is a very comprehensive procurement textbook. It will provide you with a great deal of background material that would be useful for this unit. It is presented in a clearly structured, easy-to-use format and includes many case studies and 'real world' examples to support the topics covered. It is one of the most important procurement texts available and will stand you in good stead for much of your CIPS study, including higher levels that you might progress to.

Unit content coverage

In this section we reproduce the whole of the official CIPS unit content document for this unit. The overall unit characteristics and learning outcomes for the unit are given first. Then, in the table that follows, the learning objectives and indicative content are given in the left hand column. In the right hand column are the study sessions, or subsections, in which you will find coverage of the various topics.

Unit Characteristics

This unit is designed to introduce students to the broad variety of purchasing activities. Students should be aware of the operational objectives of purchasing and the need to balance considerations of cost, lead-time and quality.

Included in the basic principles of purchasing is the need to understand the variety of key activities that purchasers are involved in, including project administration activities and contributing to the development of specifications, contact formation and the process of sourcing suppliers.

By the end of this unit, students should be able to understand the key operational processes and principles involved in the specifying, sourcing and contracting suppliers.

Learning Outcomes

On completion of this unit students should be able to:

- Identify the different types of operational objectives relevant to the purchasing function in a variety of different sectors
- Discuss the importance of the best practice relating to setting objectives within purchasing
- Contribute towards preparing supplier specifications
- Explain policy and information requirements of the organisation when preparing specifications
- Outline the stages of identifying and sourcing suppliers
- Describe the different approaches for verifying supplier information
- Identify the essential elements of a legally binding agreement

Learning objectives and indicative content

1 Identifying operational needs of the purchasing function (Weighting 25%)

1.1 Identify the differences between operational objectives in the purchasing function of a variety of different organisations including:

    • Manufacturing
    • Services
    • Retailing
    • Fast moving consumer goods (FMCG)
    • Not-for-profit
    • Processing
    • Assembly
    • Factoring and wholesaling

    Study session 1

1.2 Determine best practice in purchasing in all sectors. Right quality - quality as conformance to specification and fitness for purpose:

    • The costs of getting quality wrong,
    • Specifications quality
    • Approaches to managing supplier quality
    • The concept of zero defects

    Study session 2

1.3 Right quantity - determine the quantity required, factors influencing choice of how much to buy, minimum order levels and values:

    • Understand economic order quantities (EOQ)
    • Calculating demand
    • Concept of buffer stocks
    • Concept of insurance stocks

    Study session 3

1.4 Right place - in-bound transportation of goods to the delivery point, issues arising from UK and international transportation including:

    • Selecting transport types
    • Ensuring availability of appropriate documentation
    • Types of packaging

    Study session 4

1.5 Right time - internal, external and total lead time and factors that influence lead time, expediting, and measuring supplier delivery performance.

    • Understanding the real meaning of lead time: origination of need to fulfilment of need
    • Demand factors
    • The need for buffer stocks
    • Minimum stock levels
    • Supplier's production times
    • Logistics operator's operational systems

    Study session 5

1.6 Right price - determining the right price and appreciating the different types of costs, and the relationship to purchasing price. Study session 6
- Price elasticity
- Pricing strategies: skimming, penetration, psychological
- The concept of cost building
- The elements of cost: materials, labour, overheads, marketing, logistics and profit.
- Understanding a supplier's cost base and profit margins
- Examining what the market will bear
- Maintaining profit margins

2 Contributing towards the development of specifications (Weighting 25%) Study session 7
Study session 8

2.1 Explain the meaning of specifications and tolerances. Study session 7
- The definition of a specification
- Why it is regarded as the heart of the contract
- What are the implications of zero defects
- The need for the buyer to drive the specification
- The legal aspects of letting the supplier drive the specification

2.2 Explain the importance and purpose of developing specifications for purchasing products and services.
- Lets the supplier know that the buyer is in control
- Gives definition
- Removes doubt and the opportunity for misinterpretation
- Ensures the supplier needs to understand it is required
- to demonstrate the methodology in delivering a product or a service

2.3 Identify the different types of specification and consider the different contexts in which they are used: Study session 8

Methods	Used in sectors
• Blueprint/design	• Engineering, projects, construction
• Brand name Sample	• Small businesses, consumers
• Market grade	• Textiles, commodities
• Standards	• Commodity trades
• Performance	• Engineering, manufacturing
• Chemical/physical	• Manufacturing, electronics and most sectors
• Properties	• Chemical engineering, engineering, construction

2.4 Describe how buyers and suppliers can contribute towards effective specification development. Study session 9
- Liaison with users
- Understanding the user's needs
- Understanding the legal implications
- Minimising the tolerances

2.5 Explain information requirements for developing effective specifications -possible suppliers: Study session 10
- Technical requirements: project specifications, material specifications
- Timelines: schedules
- Delivery requirements for supply: times required

2.6 Identify areas within specifications where legislation and company policy might impact upon the development of purchasing specifications.
    • Corporate social responsibility, ethics, conflict of interest
    • Quality kite marks, processes, procedures
    • Minimum standards of practice and performance

Study session 11

3   An introduction to sourcing suppliers (Weighting 25%)

3.1 Identify the different stages of sourcing suppliers:
    • Identify the needs
    • Establish the specification
    • Survey the market
    • Source the market
    • Appraise (audit) suppliers
    • Invite quotations (tenders)
    • Analyse quotations and select the most promising supplier
    • Negotiate the best value for money
    • Award the contract
    • Monitor, review and maintain performance

Study session 12

3.2 Identify potential sources of supply and obtain information on their capabilities. Methods to be used:
    • Internet
    • Networking
    • Trade fairs and exhibitions
    • Visits from company representatives
    • Advertisements
    • Sales literature

Study session 13

3.3 Explain the pre-qualification criteria for new suppliers.
    • Financial status
    • Capacity of the company to produce
    • Technical capability
    • Adherence to systems and procedures
    • Conformance to legislation
    • The supplier's supply chain
    • The supplier's customer base
    • The culture of the company
    • The identified costs of the proposed purchase

Study session 14

3.4 Identify the different ways of verifying the information provided by suppliers including:
    • References
    • Financial assessments
    • Ability to manage high volumes
    • Delivery and quality records

Study session 15

4   An introduction to contracts for purchasing (Weighting 25%)

4.1 Provide an overview of the legal system, the sources of law:
    • The basis of the legal system in the UK and in Europe
    • The difference between statutes and case law
    • The role of parliament and the judiciary

Study session 16

4.2 Outline the key components of the formation of contract. Study session 17
- Offer
- Acceptance
- Consideration
- Intention to be legally bound
- Capacity

4.3 Explain the concept of Contract Terms and Conditions – Study session 18
expressed and implied:
- Defining terms and conditions
- Understanding the need for terms
- Examining basic terms: termination, payment, ownership, risk.

4.4 Explain privity and exceptions to the doctrine of privity: Study session 19
including Contracts, Rights of Third Parties Act 1999:
- Understanding when legal liability moves from the buyer to another party

4.5 Describe different approaches to resolving contractual disputes. Study session 20
- Negotiation
- Arbitration
- Adjudication
- Through a court of law

Study session 1
Purchasing objectives in different types of organisation

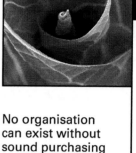

Introduction

This session will briefly examine the essential nature and purpose of purchasing and supply in different types of organisation, with particular emphasis on the basic objectives of purchasing. The intention here is to provide a basic underpinning for everything else that will follow.

No organisation can exist without sound purchasing and supply; so what is 'purchasing and supply'?

Session learning objectives

After completing this session you should be able to:

1.1 Describe the nature of different types of organisation.
1.2 Describe typical purchasing objectives in a manufacturing company.
1.3 Describe typical purchasing objectives in a service organisation.
1.4 Describe purchasing objectives in a retailing company.
1.5 Describe purchasing objectives in not-for-profit organisations such as charities.

Unit content coverage

This study session covers the following topics from the official CIPS unit content document:

Learning outcome

Identify the different types of operational objectives relevant to the purchasing function in a variety of different sectors.

Learning objective

1.1 Identify the differences between operational objectives in the purchasing function of a variety of different organisations including:
- Manufacturing
- Services
- Retailing
- Fast-moving consumer goods
- Not-for-profit
- Processing
- Assembly
- Factoring and wholesaling

Timing

You should set aside about 3¼ hours to read and complete this session, including learning activities, self-assessment questions, the suggested further reading (if any) and the revision question.

1

1.1 The nature of different types of organisation

There are many different types of organisation, each of which operates in different ways and which will have different types of objective. It is important to be aware of these differences because they will play a major role in shaping how the organisation develops policies and how it operates. These objectives, in turn, will to a great extent dictate how the purchasing and supply function operates and what its goals and objectives are.

Knowledge of how organisations operate will underpin all of the remainder of this unit.

Learning activity 1.1

Try to gain an overview of different types of organisation from the text. How would you categorise the organisation you work for? For example, is it a manufacturer or some other type of organisation? Note down why you chose this designation.

Feedback on page 10

We shall now briefly examine the basic nature of a range of different types of organisation, as follows:

- **Manufacturing, including assembly**: manufacturing is about making products. Examples include complex products such as cars, televisions as well as 'simpler' things such as brooms, garden rakes and pens. Usually manufacturers buy all of the parts (or 'components') that they need and assemble them into the final product. Increasingly, manufacturers purchase sub-assemblies: that is, several components already assembled into a major part of the finished product – for example a car manufacturer buying gearboxes already assembled from a gearbox supplier rather than purchasing all of the components for the gearbox and assembling it itself.
- **Services**: organisations that provide services to either individuals or to other organisations. These are often of a specialist nature and, by definition, are intangible. They include banking, IT support, insurance and legal expertise, all of which are usually labelled 'professional' services, and more 'everyday' activities such as cleaning, catering and security.
- **Retailing ('shops')**: companies that provide 'finished goods' to 'end consumers'. The range of goods sold by retailers is enormous but would include foodstuffs, stationery products, electrical goods such as radios and telephones, and clothes. You will be able to think of many more types of shop/retailer. Retailers range in size from small corner shops to giant supermarkets and include shops of a specialist nature selling such products as books. We can include fast-moving consumer goods (FMCG) here. These are items that people need almost daily such as foodstuffs and toiletries.
- **Not-for-profit**: examples include charities and religious establishments. Such organisations look after the interests of specific groups of people or specific causes rather than the general public.

1

- **Processing**: this differs from manufacturing in that it does not involve components or assembly of a finished product. Processing usually involves starting with several ingredients that are transformed in some way, usually by cooking, fermentation or some other kind of natural process, into a finished product. Examples include brewing and bread making. The production of gas, electricity and drinking water, although different in nature from brewing and bread making, would also be included under this heading.
- **Factoring and wholesaling**: organisations under this heading are intermediaries between producers of either manufactured products or processed products and retailers. They usually specialise in a particular product type, for example electrical goods. They buy these in large quantities from manufacturers and sell them in smaller but still relatively large quantities to retailers, who then sell them in small quantities to the end consumer.

Self-assessment question 1.1

Question 1. Which of the following types of organisation does not need to make a profit?

1 car manufacturer
2 supermarket
3 charity
4 FMCG

Question 2. Which of the following types of organisation produces a finished product by assembling components?

1 wholesaling
2 manufacturing
3 processing
4 services

Question 3. Which of the following types of organisation provides intangible benefits to the general public?

1 services
2 not-for-profit
3 retailing
4 processing

Feedback on page 10

1.2 Purchasing objectives in a manufacturing company

Learning activity 1.2

You have recently been appointed purchasing manager for a manufacturer of televisions, DVD players and other electrical items. To get a 'feel' for

(continued on next page)

1

Learning activity 1.2 *(continued)*

the job you decide to find out what the main factors that affect the role of purchasing in this company are. To provide a starting point, write down what you would consider the major factors about the company and its processes that might have a direct bearing on purchasing.

Feedback on page 10

Manufacturing involves the assembly of components into a finished product. Its main purchases will therefore be the components required to make the finished product. This might sound easy but there are several considerations that you need to be aware of:

- **Product complexity**: many finished products are extremely complex, a good example being cars, which would contain over 1,000 different components.
- **Sub-assemblies**: many manufacturers purchase sub-assemblies, and some products are manufactured entirely out of these, for example the Smart car, which is assembled entirely from about 12 major sub-assemblies such as engine, gearbox, body and so on.
- **Quality**: very important! The quality of the finished product will be highly dependent on the quality of purchased components and sub-assemblies. This places great onus on the buyer to ensure that suppliers are capable of supplying goods of the right quality and can supply that quality on a continuing basis.
- **The need for continual re-supply**: many manufacturers produce their product in large quantities, sometimes hundreds or even thousands per week. It is not possible to store all of the components and sub-assemblies required for this volume of production and so suppliers must supply relatively small quantities frequently. This is a process sometimes known as **just-in-time (JIT)** and places great emphasis on ensuring that the buyer has suppliers that can provide this level of service and continue to provide it over time.
- **Non-production purchases**: there are other purchases, apart from components and sub-assemblies, required just to keep the company operating. This type of purchase is usually known as **maintenance, repair and operational (MRO)** and involves such items as stationery, janitorial supplies, lubricants and safety equipment. MRO supplies are required by all organisations, no matter what their main activity.
- **Computer-controlled processes**: many major manufacturers have computer-based processes that control the production flow and hence the purchasing requirements, for example **material requirements planning (MRP)**, which identifies when components and sub-assemblies need reordering and in what quantities.
- **Services**: as with many other types of organisation most manufacturers purchase a range of services as well as production components and so on. Many of these services would be fairly mundane, such as catering and cleaning, but some would be of a specialist nature, such as design work.
- **Capital items**: buyers in manufacturing companies will often have to purchase pieces of equipment used to support the production process in some way, such as robot welding machines. Such large, expensive, purchases are known as capital items and require a different purchasing

approach from day-to-day purchases, usually involving a committee to agree on designs and to appraise potential suppliers as well as highly detailed contracts. The purchasing of capital items will be examined elsewhere in your studies.

Self-assessment question 1.2

Question 1. What are individual parts that go together to make a finished product called?

1 components
2 sub-assemblies
3 MRO supplies
4 capital goods.

Question 2. In a manufacturing company, which of the following is likely to be the major type of purchase?

1 MRO items
2 raw materials and components
3 capital goods
4 services.

Question 3. Which of the following best describes capital goods?

1 Individual parts that go together to make the finished product.
2 Large pieces of equipment, such as machinery, that make the production process possible.
3 Items that are required to keep the company in operation.
4 Components assembled together to form a large part of the finished product.

Feedback on page 10

1.3 Typical purchasing objectives in a service organisation

In this section we need to consider both public and private sectors.

Typical services include financial services and insurance in the private sector, and healthcare and education in the public sector, although these examples are by no means exhaustive.

Goods and services that might be purchased by a service organisation may include (depending on the nature of the service provided):

- office equipment and stationery
- utilities (gas, electricity, water)
- computer equipment and software packages
- maintenance services
- specialist services such as advertising and design services
- uniforms

1

- travel
- printing services
- vehicles.

You should be able to see that many of these goods and services are crucial in terms of supporting 'mainstream' staff in performing their various duties. You should also notice that some of the items on the list, such as office equipment and vehicles, would be classed as capital equipment. It is equally important that these items and services are available at the time and place required and that both services and material purchases are of the right quality.

Also buyers in service organisations will have to purchase MRO items, usually stationery and office consumables, although some items such as safety equipment may be required in some organisations.

Learning activity 1.3

Reflect on your reading of the text and perhaps your own experiences and try to write down the similarities and differences between purchasing for a jobcentre and for a chain of hairdressers.

Feedback on page 11

You should now move on to the following self-assessment question.

Self-assessment question 1.3

Identify what you regard as being the main differences and similarities between purchasing in a service organisation and purchasing in a manufacturing organisation.

Feedback on page 11

1.4 Typical purchasing objectives in a retail organisation including FMCG

The nature of this type of organisation is different from others in that there is no transformation of goods taking place. Finished goods are sold to end consumers without being changed or processed in any way.

The main aspect of purchasing here is the need to maintain a flow of finished goods into the organisation and its various branches. This situation is particularly difficult when you realise that many goods in (for example) supermarkets are perishable in nature and must, therefore, be purchased on a continuous basis similar to JIT. Examples here include fresh fruit and vegetables. These cannot be frozen and will not keep for very long in stock (about 12 hours maximum). This problem is compounded by the fact that large supermarket chains have dozens if not hundreds of branches – the

1

leading UK supermarket chain, Tesco, has around 700 branches – and that purchasing is usually performed centrally. Buyers are faced, therefore, with the pressure of ensuring that they have suppliers who are capable of maintaining *daily* deliveries to several branches.

Learning activity 1.4

Visit your local supermarket and note down how many main product categories there are (for example by looking at the overhead signs in the aisles). Take the category of butter, margarine and spreads and count how many different makes are stocked including 'own brand'. Suggest how the purchasing department might be organised to ensure that the shelves are fully stocked at all times.

Feedback on page 11

Large supermarket chains have great purchasing power and are often able to negotiate very low prices. Supermarkets often sell products such as tinned food and breakfast cereals under their own brand name alongside the more well-known brands. These products are purchased from the manufacturers of the branded product but are usually sold at a lower price than the better-known branded products, placing on the buyer the onus of negotiating very low prices but at the same time maintaining acceptable quality levels.

The high levels of spend and the large variety that is often found in product categories in supermarkets mean that there is often a very high degree of product specialisation in supermarket purchasing. This is magnified by the fact that, in the retail sector in general, purchasing and marketing are effectively the same function because retailers buy what they can sell.

FMCG

Much of the above applies to FMCG companies but the following are worthy of particular attention:

*   They are items sold very frequently because customers have frequent demand for them. Examples of FMCG include foodstuffs and toiletries.
*   They tend to be sold across the whole country and increasingly, across entire regions of the world such as EU.
*   Consistency of quality.
*   Consistency of supply.
*   Branding and packaging: FMCG usually have a strong brand image (think Coca-Cola or similar) and packaging carrying a brand 'message' can contribute to this. Such packaging needs to be purchased and the buyer needs to have good, reliable suppliers in this area.

General

As with any other kind of organisation there will be a requirement for the purchase of MRO items and capital goods. There will usually be less

1

emphasis on the purchase of services or outsourcing, with the possible exception of transport, which is a service that is often purchased by supermarket chains.

Self-assessment question 1.4

You are the purchasing manager of a large retail organisation that has recently employed a buyer whose background is in manufacturing industry. The buyer has frequently made the comment that, to perform their role successfully, all they need to do is to use the skills they acquired in the manufacturing sector. You are concerned about this approach because you believe that the retail sector is very different from the manufacturing sector.

Write a brief report to the buyer indicating what you see as being the main differences between purchasing in a retail organisation and purchasing in other types of organisation, particularly manufacturing.

Feedback on page 12

1.5   Purchasing objectives in not-for-profit organisations

Examples of such organisations include charities, churches (in the collective sense such as the Church of England) and other religious bodies, and organisations such as museums.

Although not making profits, if these organisations keep to a minimum their expenditure on required goods and services, a greater percentage of donations received can be used to support the organisation's cause. In the case of religious bodies, if such expenditure is minimised, income can be used to preserve or improve the fabric of buildings. In the case of museums, minimising expenditure in this way can mean that the quality and range of items on display can be maintained and improved.

Increasingly, rather than trying to rely exclusively on donations, many of the above types of organisation sell products, for example gifts, clothing and souvenirs, income from whose sale will contribute to the work of the organisation. This means that buyers working in such organisations need to ensure that such products are purchased at a price that will allow a 'profit' to be made that can be used to support the objectives of the organisation, such as a good cause, building fabric, and so on. Also, the quality of goods purchased for this type of resale needs to be adequate to attract people to buy them.

A further consideration is the need to make such products as these 'distinctive': for example, the products sold by one charity need to be distinctive from the products sold by another.

Thus buyers in this type of organisation need to be able to negotiate relatively low prices for goods of reasonable quality that will be sold in relatively low quantities, a combination that does not give the buyer much purchasing power. This potential problem can be alleviated to some extent when charities work together in the way that, for example, some UK animal-based charities do, such as the RSPCA, PDSA, League Against Cruel Sports and so on.

Learning activity 1.5

Try to find an example of a charity gift catalogue. Put yourself in the position of the charity's purchasing director and note down what you see as being the key issues you need to tackle to ensure the catalogue's success.

Feedback on page 12

You should now move on to the following self-assessment question.

Self-assessment question 1.5

You have recently taken up a post with a major national charity, having previously spent most of your work time in the retail sector. Discuss the opportunities and challenges that you and the charity are likely to face.

Feedback on page 12

Revision question

Now try the revision question for this session on page 195.

Summary

This session was concerned with different types of purchasing environment, all of which have some similarities. For example, all organisations will need to purchase maintenance, repair and operational items (MRO), and consumables such as stationery. However, different types of organisation will require different purchases for their key operation(s) such as:

- Manufacturing: raw materials and components.
- Retail/FMCG: finished goods.
- Not-for-profit: maintenance items and services and goods for gift catalogues, where applicable.
- Service: materials to support the service.

You should now have a sound knowledge of these major differences.

Suggested further reading

You might like to read more about these topics in chapter 3 of Baily et al (2004).

1

Feedback on learning activities and self-assessment questions

Feedback on learning activity 1.1

You probably categorised your organisation as one of the following:

- manufacturing
- services
- retailing
- fast-moving consumer goods (FMCG)
- not-for-profit
- processing
- assembly
- factoring and wholesaling.

Read the detailed descriptions of these types of organisation in the remainder of the section and check that your categorisation is correct. When you have finished reading, think about whether you categorisation is correct, whether you would change it, or whether it fits into more than one category.

Feedback on self-assessment question 1.1

Question 1: the correct answer is 3.

Question 2: the correct answer is 2.

Question 3: the correct answer is 1.

Feedback on learning activity 1.2

A difficult one, but the kinds of issue you should have identified would be:

- The product is complex.
- Quality is very important.
- Sub-assemblies form a major part of the production process and therefore, of purchasing.
- The need for materials to keep the company going (**maintenance repair and operational**, MRO).
- The need for constant re-supply.
- Computer-controlled systems to control reordering.
- Capital purchases.
- The purchase of services.

Feedback on self-assessment question 1.2

Question 1: the correct answer is 2.

Question 2: the correct answer is 2.

Question 3: the correct answer is 2.

Feedback on learning activity 1.3

There is no prescriptive list here but you should have identified some of the following:

Similarities:

- Energy.
- Support services (for example cleaning in both, IT support in the jobcentre and accounting in the hairdressers).
- Support materials, for example shampoo, razors and so on for the hairdressers and stationery for the jobcentre.
- MRO items.

Differences:

The differences are more likely to be differences in the actual nature of purchases rather than purchase categories. For example, a jobcentre would probably find that stationery is a major purchase whereas the hairdressers would not, although in both cases it would be classed as support materials. Also, the jobcentre would require more specialist services such as HR and IT support than would the hairdressers.

Feedback on self-assessment question 1.3

The differences you should have identified are that purchasing in a service organisation will be concerned more with the purchasing of services or outsourcing and that manufacturing purchases such as components and raw materials will not be purchased at all in a service organisation. Another difference is that, in a service organisation, purchases are made largely to support the staff who actually provide the service.

Similarities are that MRO purchases and capital purchases will be required in both types of organisation.

Feedback on learning activity 1.4

The number of product categories and individual brands of butter and so on depends on the supermarket chain in question, but you would expect to find around 100 product categories and around 50 brands of butter, margarine, spreads and so on.

Purchasing would ensure that shelves are kept stocked by:

- Systems to forecast requirements. There is a system called electronic point of sale or EPOS, which operates through the checkout machines and gives a perpetual automatic reading of stocks remaining after customers have made purchases, that provides such information.
- Close liaison with marketing.
- Reliable transport.

Feedback on self-assessment question 1.4

The main areas you should have considered would be:

- The fact that goods purchased for a retail organisation are sold to the end consumer without being processed or transformed in any way.
- There is usually a higher degree of product specialisation by buyers in retail organisations than in other organisations.
- Retail organisations such as supermarkets use a sophisticated system known as EPOS to drive the re-supply process that is required for most product categories.
- Buyers in retail organisations have a much closer liaison with marketing than do buyers in other types of organisation.
- The need to purchase 'own brand' products is not usually found in other types of organisation.
- Very quick response times are needed because many sales (and therefore, purchases) are at the whim of the customer.

Feedback on learning activity 1.5

The kinds of issue you should have focused on would be:

- Quality: is it sufficient to attract purchasers?
- Variety: is it also sufficient to attract purchasers?
- Are the products distinctive from other charity catalogues?
- Are the products distinctive from high street shops?
- Are pricing levels too high to attract purchasers?
- Are they high enough to allow funds to go to the 'cause'?

Feedback on self-assessment question 1.5

This is a broad task. The overall nature of the challenge would be to ensure that the cost of purchases was kept to a minimum to allow the upkeep of the actual operation and at the same time allow enough surplus funds to provide support for the chosen 'cause'.

A major issue is that of perceived 'profit': a charity would probably acquire adverse publicity if it gained a reputation for driving down suppliers' profits to an unreasonable level in order to make a 'profit'.

An opportunity is that, where gift catalogues are concerned, there seems to be more willingness on the part of the public to buy gifts rather than make donations. This could be capitalised on by sound purchasing.

Obtaining the right quality

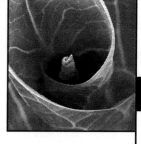

Introduction

This session is concerned with the achievement of good quality in products and services, and is based very much on the premise that your organisation cannot provide good quality products or services to its customers without good quality supplies from its suppliers. Good quality is achieved largely by liaison between technical staff and purchasing staff, with purchasing staff potentially having an important role to play in achieving good quality. This session is devoted largely to examining this role of purchasing staff, although to start with we need to examine the, sometimes thorny, issue of what constitutes good quality. Towards the end of the session we shall examine how we can manage suppliers to ensure that they provide us with good quality, as well as examining some of the newer approaches to quality such as 'zero defects'.

'Quality in a product or service is not what the supplier puts in. It is what the customer gets out and is willing to pay for...'
Peter F Drucker

Session learning objectives

After completing this session you should be able to:

2.1 Define quality as either 'conformance to specification' or 'fitness for purpose'.
2.2 Explain the costs involved in getting the right quality as well as in getting quality wrong.
2.3 Explain the principles of managing supplier quality.

Unit content coverage

This study session covers the following topics from the official CIPS unit content document:

Learning outcome

Discuss the importance of the best practice relating to setting objectives within purchasing.

Learning objective

1.2 Determine best practice in purchasing in all sectors.
Right quality – quality as conformance to specification and fitness for purpose:
 • The costs of getting quality wrong
 • Specifications quality

2

- Approaches to managing supplier quality
- The concept of zero defects.

Prior knowledge

None specific but session 1 should prove useful in establishing the context.

Timing

You should set aside about 2¼ hours to read and complete this session, including learning activities, self-assessment questions, the suggested further reading (if any) and the revision question.

2.1 Quality as either 'conformance to specification' or 'fitness for purpose'

Quality is not an 'absolute' and can be defined, broadly speaking, in either of the above ways.

People think of quality in different ways. Most 'personal' views on quality are subjective: think 'luxury image', for example Mercedes cars. In business and commerce we need more objective (measurable, specific) means of defining quality. Essentially, there are two commonly used business-related definitions:

- quality is 'conformance to specification'
- quality is 'fitness for purpose'.

Learning activity 2.1

When you are at work, look at the type of specifications your organisation uses. If necessary enlist the help of other people, perhaps technical departments or other user departments. Write down and keep a record of whether your organisation uses conformance or performance specifications and why your organisation uses the particular type of specification it does. If necessary ask other personnel this question and record the answer.

If your organisation uses a mixture of conformance and performance specifications, try to find out why and record the answer.

Feedback on page 20

'Conformance to specification' describes quality as getting a product or service that does what was specified. The means of transmitting such requirements are known as **conformance specifications** and are seen as emphasising inputs and limiting suppliers' freedom. The buyer details precisely what is required, and it could be that the use to which the material or service is to be put is never known by the supplier. The main advantage of conformance specifications is that they allow the buyer to keep tight control over the quality of supplied materials.

'Fitness for purpose' describes quality in terms of whether the product or service does what is required, and is usually known as a **performance specification.** These emphasise outputs and are seen as encouraging supplier innovation. The basic objective of a performance specification is that the supplier provides something that is **fit for the purpose** required. Many buyers prefer to use performance specifications and their advantages will be examined in study session 8.

In some cases it may be appropriate to use a mixture of performance and conformance specifications.

Self-assessment question 2.1

In the text you will have read that sometimes an overall specification for a particular requirement might be a combination of conformance and performance specifications. Such a combination of specifications might be those for a catering service for a works canteen, for example.

Take a works canteen catering service as an example and list three conformance specifications and three performance specifications that you might include in your overall specification.

Feedback on page 20

2.2 The costs involved in getting quality wrong

The 'right' quality was considered in section 2.1 above. The right quality at the right price gives good value, but if we get the quality wrong it can cost us more than it should because of possible unnecessary costs resulting from:

- Over-specification: usually this means specifying a material that is better than it needs to be to fulfil the purpose, or specifying tolerances that are too tight. Tolerances are explained in study session 7.
- Under-specification: specifying something that is simply not good enough for the purpose required. The usual reason for doing this is to try to get away with paying a lower price for the item. Unfortunately, the likely consequence of this course of action is that the item does not perform its required function adequately. This can lead to costs resulting from the organisation not being able to perform its work satisfactorily, or not at all, and/or costs resulting from inferior items or materials causing damage to, for example, machines.
- The supplier failing to conform to the specification: this tends to be a problem relating particularly to conformance specifications and can be rectified, largely, by the use of performance specifications. If conformance specifications must be used, the potential problem can

2

be resolved only by ensuring that only suppliers that are known to be capable of performing in accordance with specifications are selected.
- Unclear or incorrect specifications that might result in disruption and delays to provision of the product or service (for example, caused by time spent providing additional information and clarification).

Learning activity 2.2

Think about products and services that you have purchased that you feel were under- or over-specified, or where the supplier failed to conform to the specification. Write down:

- what costs resulted from this
- how these costs were incurred
- how the purchasing department could have helped to prevent this situation from occurring.

Feedback on page 21

This leads us to:

Different costs of quality

There are said to be three costs of quality, each of which occurs at a different stage in the life of a product or material:

- cost of prevention
- cost of detection
- cost of rectification.

Traditionally, not too much attention was paid to the cost of prevention, the emphasis being to *detect* faults once a product had been made (inspection) and then *rectify* any faults identified. Recently, people have realised that it is cheaper overall to put more effort into *prevention* of faults in the first place so that less detection and rectification of faults is needed later on. Achieving this means paying more attention to the specification process than was traditionally the case and ensuring that specifications are written to achieve good quality. This concept of *costs of quality* is something that you will examine in more detail later in your CIPS studies.

Roles of buyer and seller in quality/specifications

These will be explained in study session 9.

Self-assessment question 2.2

You are a purchasing manager and you are concerned that some of your staff do not appear to realise that purchasing staff have a part to play in ensuring quality and writing specifications, believing that such activities are solely the domain of technical staff.

(continued on next page)

Self-assessment question 2.2 *(continued)*

Draft a report to your staff outlining what you believe to be the role of purchasing staff in determining quality and writing specifications.

Feedback on page 21

2.3 Introduction to the principles of managing supplier quality

The concept of *managing* suppliers' quality is relatively new but is essentially a combination of quality assurance and quality control, as we shall see.

There are two distinct aspects to quality (see section 2.1 above):

- quality of design
- quality of conformance to design.

Quality of design encompasses all activities that are planned in advance of a process to ensure that what is produced will be fit for its purpose. This process is often known as 'quality assurance' or QA. It plays a large part in quality management. Quality control or QC, on the other hand, is concerned largely with process conformance issues.

Quality control

This typically involves inspection at the goods inward department, where inspectors check samples, or in some cases *all* of the inputs received from suppliers. Defective items are separated out and discarded, assuming some allowance for failure is permitted in the contract. Alternatively, defective parts are returned to suppliers for credit or are rectified at the supplier's expense. Goods received should be quarantined, and not issued until they have been inspected, passed and certified by the inspection department.

This system has several inherent drawbacks.

- It is expensive and time-consuming, and means that more storage space is required.
- It does not necessarily lead to an improvement in quality. In many cases, particularly if sampling is relied upon, defective products would filter through.
- There is a limit to the extent to which quality can be 'inspected in' at this stage. Some items can only be partially tested because, if properly tested, they would be destroyed (for example, fire extinguishers).
- There is little incentive for suppliers to improve quality or perform checks if they know that their customer will do it for them.
- It is arguable that the best person to initially check for faults in a product is the person who has made it. Suppliers should be experts in their own products.

Quality assurance

Quality assurance is concerned with defect prevention and includes design, specification, supplier assessment, and education and training of users and suppliers. The basic objective of quality assurance is to ensure that all products are manufactured free from defects, conform to all specifications, and satisfy the customer's requirements. Quality assurance is a proactive process whereas quality control is reactive.

Quality management

Essentially, this is a combination of the two processes already mentioned with the addition of some other concepts, and can be described as follows:

- Ensuring that we have specifications that indicate our quality requirements.
- Ensuring that we have quality-capable suppliers. This will be covered in depth in study session 13. A good starting point for ensuring that you have quality-capable suppliers is to select ones that are accredited to ISO 9000:2000. Many buyers use this accreditation as a minimum pre-qualification criterion for supplier selection, and you will encounter it in more detail in later CIPS studies.
- Monitoring suppliers' quality performance on an ongoing basis. This will involve inspection at the goods inward department as well as 'in-process'. This latter is the occasional inspection of a supplier's production process with the objective of monitoring the supplier's own inspection measures.
- In some cases, it will be sufficient to rely on the supplier to produce the product or deliver the service to the right quality. This might be the case where:
  - The consequences of failure of the product or service are negligible.
  - The buyer has approved the supplier's quality system.
  - The supplier has a proven capability over time.

Zero defects

Both quality control and quality assurance have the potential drawback that some defective material might be allowed to 'slip through the net' causing problems either on the production line or, even worse, if defective material reaches end consumers. In recognition of such possibilities, some quality experts, notably Philip B Crosby, have developed the concept of zero defects.

Zero defects takes the view that *no defects* are acceptable and that systems that potentially allow defects to occur are not satisfactory. It is likely to increase the costs of prevention of faults but savings resulting from reduced costs of detection and rectification (see section 2.2 above) should outweigh any such increase in costs.

In terms of material coming from outside suppliers, zero defects can be implemented by ensuring that suppliers have absorbed the message of zero defects and are committed to its goals, and by the increased monitoring of suppliers' processes.

There are specific techniques that can be used to make a zero defects approach possible such as failure mode and effects analysis (FMEA). You will examine this in detail later in your CIPS studies. However, in brief, it

2

is a system that involves examining a process and identifying any aspect of it that is likely to fail, starting with aspects that are *highly likely* to fail and working through to aspects that are *hardly likely* to fail. Action is then taken to prevent all of these potential failures from occurring before they actually do occur, thus giving a defect-free process, which, in essence, *is* zero defects.

In summary, the benefits that can be gained from a zero defects approach to quality management are:

- Reduced total quality costs: increased costs of prevention being outweighed by reduced costs of detection and rectification.
- Reduced likelihood of damage to the production line due to defective materials being processed or assembled.
- Reduced likelihood of costs of recalling finished products from end consumers due to material or component defects.
- Reduced likelihood of adverse publicity due to defective finished products reaching end consumers.

Learning activity 2.3

1 Using your own experience and/or through discussion with work colleagues note down the methods or systems used to manage the quality of supplies. If they are different from those described in this section, outline what they are.
2 If your organisation uses the zero defects approach, note down:
   (a) how this is achieved
   (b) what benefits it achieves.
3 If your organisation does not use the zero defects approach, identify:
   (a) what benefits it could bring
   (b) why it has not been implemented nor would not be.

Feedback on page 21

Now that you have completed the learning activity, see if you can answer this question:

Self-assessment question 2.3

As a purchasing manager, draft a report to your line manager indicating how you would best approach the management of supplier quality. Use your own organisation as a model, if you wish.

Feedback on page 22

Revision question

Now try the revision question for this session on page 195.

2

Summary

In this session we have considered some important aspects of quality, including:

- the specifying of quality requirements
- the costs of quality including the costs associated with getting quality wrong
- quality control, quality assurance and quality management.

Quality is one of the most important aspects of purchasing and supply, and you must recognise that the ability of your organisation to provide a good quality product or service depends greatly upon the quality of supplied material.

We shall return to the subject of specifications and consider them in more detail in study sessions 7 – 11.

Suggested further reading

You can read about quality and specifications in much more detail in chapter 9 of Lysons and Farrington (2006).

Feedback on learning activities and self-assessment questions

Feedback on learning activity 2.1

There is no specific feedback because the answers will depend entirely on the nature of your organisation and its needs. Typical answers might be that an organisation uses conformance specifications because it wants to keep a tight reign on quality, or that it uses performance specifications because it has a range of suppliers that it considers innovative and trustworthy and wants to encourage their technical input into purchased materials and goods.

Feedback on self-assessment question 2.1

Conformance specifications might include:

- Must offer a vegetarian choice.
- Must open at 7.00 a.m. daily.
- Must sterilise all work surfaces three times a day.
- Must have a take-away service as well as a sit-down service.
- Must have a certain number of tables and seats.

Performance specifications might include:

- Food to be tasty (measured by consumer survey, complaints box, etc).
- No more than 10 minutes' waiting time at peak times.
- All complaints to be dealt with and resolved within, for example, 48 hours.

2

- Changes to the menu or special requirements for VIP guests to be put into operation when required.

You should note that this list is not exhaustive, and you may be able to think of some other points that are not listed here.

Feedback on learning activity 2.2

There is no specific feedback because of the personal nature of the activity, but costs identified would typically be:

- Costs arising from rectification/replacement. Normally this would be done at the supplier's expense if they were in the wrong, but there are still the costs of inspection and so on.
- Costs arising from the item not being good enough to perform its required function.
- Costs of over-specification; sometimes it becomes apparent that a cheaper item with a lesser specification will do the job just as well.

It would be useful if you were able to identify any costs arising that were not mentioned in the text, although any such costs would probably be of a 'knock on' nature. These might include transport costs involved in returning faulty materials to the supplier, although the supplier should be liable for these, but this depends on the terms and conditions of the contract with the supplier.

Feedback on self-assessment question 2.2

Typical areas you should have covered are:

- The need to minimise total quality costs: discussion of the various costs of quality would be useful here.
- The need to ensure that, where possible, items are specified that are readily available in supply markets, and that items do not need to be custom-made unless absolutely necessary.
- Ensuring, where possible, that specifications are not under- or over-specified. Some buyers would argue that they do not possess the necessary knowledge to do this, but standard supply market specifications, which should be known to buyers, should act as a guide.
- Making users aware of possible alternatives to items they have specified.

Feedback on learning activity 2.3

There is no specific feedback here because of the individual nature of the activity. However, a possible alternative approach to managing supplier quality would be the use of third-party assessors such as the Swiss company SGS, or taking the view that, if suppliers produce in line with certain recognised standards such as ISO 9000:2000, their goods will be accepted.

Zero defects can be achieved by ensuring that suppliers are committed to its goals and have systems to achieve it, and its main benefits are reduced quality costs and better quality finished products that will 'delight' the end consumer.

2

It is difficult to know why zero defects might not be used apart from organisational lethargy. Some service organisations might say its place is in manufacturing and that it has no role for service providers, but, with thought, it can be modified to suit this environment.

Feedback on self-assessment question 2.3

If you use your own organisation as a model, your answer will be, in some respects individual. However, you should discuss such issues as:

- Quality assurance: it is better to try to prevent defects than to identify them and rectify them later.
- Quality control: may still be useful but can be expensive and still allow defects through.
- The need to perform supplier appraisal.
- Zero defects and how it could be achieved.

Obtaining the right quantity

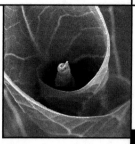

Introduction

Are you buying too much material, not enough, or the right quantity? How do you know?

Along with the other 'rights' of purchasing, it is important for purchasing and supply staff to ensure that the right quantity of goods or materials is purchased. In this session we shall examine the methods available to purchasing staff to ensure that the 'right' quantity is purchased, as well as some of the considerations that may affect this decision-making process. We shall also link demand and how it might be calculated to this process.

Session learning objectives

After completing this session you should be able to:

3.1 Describe how to determine the quantity of goods/materials required, and explain the factors influencing the choice of how much to buy.
3.2 Explain the effect of minimum order quantities and values.
3.3 Explain the concept of economic order quantities (EOQ) and describe how to calculate them.
3.4 Identify methods of stock replenishment and the need for and methods of calculation of buffer stocks.

Unit content coverage

This study session covers the following topics from the official CIPS unit content document:

Learning outcome

Discuss the importance of the best practice relating to setting objectives within purchasing.

Learning objective

1.3 Right quantity: determine the quantity required, factors influencing choice of how much to buy, minimum order levels and values:
* Understand economic order quantities (EOQ)
* Calculating demand
* Concept of buffer stocks
* Concept of insurance stocks

Prior knowledge

None although sessions 1 and 2 will 'set the scene' to some extent.

3

Timing

You should set aside about 3¾ hours to read and complete this session, including learning activities, self-assessment questions, the suggested further reading (if any) and the revision question.

3.1 How to determine the quantity of goods or materials required, including determining demand factors

Many buyers would say that the actual quantity of an item or material to be purchased is a matter for the user department, and that purchasing and supply staff have no role to play in this process. This may be true, but there are situations where buyers can influence the quantity to be purchased for very good reasons, such as being able to obtain a better deal from a supplier. To be able to exert such influence, buyers need to know how quantities might be calculated, and must have some awareness of demand patterns.

In some cases, the quantity required is straightforward. For example, if replacing a worn-out forklift truck, the quantity will be one. However, in many cases, the right order quantity requires significant thought.

Learning activity 3.1

Identify how you calculate quantities to be purchased in your workplace and compare them with the principles given in the text that follows. Try to identify any differences and similarities and make a note of them.

Feedback on page 32

Quantity calculation in different types of organisation

Examples include:

- A retailer buying stock for sale may have a stock planning and control system to determine what is stocked and in what quantity. For example, a supermarket's electronic point of sale (EPOS) system (see study session 1) will automatically calculate when it is necessary to reorder a product, and the quantity stocked, and therefore ordered, will be determined by the company's marketing and sales policy.
- A manufacturing company may have a production planning and control system to determine the requirements for parts and materials to support production, which, in turn, will be based on the forecasted demand for sales of the finished product. Many manufacturers use IT-based systems such as material requirements planning (MRP) to calculate such demand for purchased materials and components.

You should note that all organisations would need to purchase consumables, and maintenance, repair and operational (MRO) items. The quantities of these items to be purchased would be calculated separately.

Other organisations, such as those in the service sector, will usually buy the quantity necessary to fulfil a particular need when that need is identified.

3

Suppliers' effect on quantities to be purchased

It may appear worth buying more than is actually required to get a cheaper price through bulk discount. However, the impact of buying larger quantities is that stock will increase and with it the costs associated with holding stock.

The benefit of bulk discounts needs to be balanced against increased stockholding costs, and the buyer should work with those who establish the quantities required (for example, stock and production planning functions) to establish the optimum purchase quantity.

Some suppliers have minimum order quantities (MOQ) or values, and we shall examine these in section 3.2.

In many organisations the products or services they sell have seasonal demand, and demand forecasts need to take this into account. Examples include, among others:

- garden tools and barbecue equipment
- painting and decorating supplies
- Christmas cards and wrapping paper.

Stock replenishment systems, where stock is reordered when the amount of stock reaches the reorder level, require an estimate of future demand.

Companies producing highly capital-intensive items such as planes, ships, trains or engines would produce only to customer demand. This can remove the need for forecasting. In most industries, though, there is a need to forecast sales because the organisation's production will depend on forecasted demand. In practice, many suppliers will stock both to known customer orders and to their forecasts. When organisations produce to known customer orders, demand for material stocks for productions and operations will be *dependent* on these customer orders.

Self-assessment question 3.1

Using your own organisation, or one with which you are familiar, write a report on the considerations that will help determine how quantities of purchased materials should be calculated.

Feedback on page 32

3.2 Minimum order quantities (MOQ)

Some suppliers, particularly those that sell small finished goods in relatively large quantities, impose an MOQ. Typically items that fall under this heading have a very low unit price, and examples might include:

- fasteners (nuts and bolts, and others)
- janitorial supplies
- some stationery products
- lubricants.

The reason for this is that, if they supply small quantities of their product in the normal way with full accompanying paperwork (order acknowledgement, advice note, invoice and so on), the cost of administration outweighs the value of the order. Such suppliers then set the MOQ at a level that ensures that the value of the order is greater than the cost of processing it.

An alternative to the MOQ, but one that has much the same effect, is the minimum order value, which will be calculated to be a figure that outweighs the cost of processing an order.

Learning activity 3.2

If you are faced with a supplier's MOQ what, if anything, would you do about it? Try asking colleagues what they feel could be done about it. Compare your answer with the text that follows.

Feedback on page 33

What action can the buyer take over MOQ?

First, you need to decide whether a particular MOQ is a problem; it might not be. If it is a problem then you need to think about what course of action to take.

Generally, there is not much you can do: if you want a quantity that is less than the supplier's MOQ or minimum order value, you have to buy the MOQ or the quantity represented by the minimum order value. There should be no real problem with this course of action if the following considerations apply:

- The quantity of the item will be used in due course.
- You have adequate storage space for the item until the quantity is used.
- The item will not deteriorate in storage.
- The item is not likely to be prone to theft or pilferage while in store.

If the considerations listed above do not apply, you are looking at wasting money because you will simply be buying a quantity larger than is required and, in effect, throwing away the unused items. However, there may be no alternative, meaning that you have to buy the large quantity knowing that there will be waste. Possible ways of avoiding the situation might include:

- If the item is perishable, but you will use the MOQ at some point, try to negotiate with the supplier that, even if you pay the price of the MOQ 'upfront', they will supply the item in quantities that you actually need at times spread throughout the year.
- Try to find another supplier, although this is often easier said than done!
- Discuss the requirement with the user to identify whether it can be changed to something that may be purchased without an MOQ.

3

Self-assessment question 3.2

You have a manager of a user department who insists that you ignore MOQ so that the department can be sure of having the required items. You want the manager to consider using something different to avoid the MOQ possibility.

Prepare a plan for discussing the matter with the manager, indicating the arguments that you would use to try to convince the manager that MOQ is a bad thing.

Feedback on page 33

3.3 Economic order quantity and how to calculate it

One way of ensuring that you buy the right quantity of material or items is to use the economic order quantity (EOQ) calculation. EOQ seeks to calculate an order quantity based on the minimum **acquisition cost** to the company, taking account of:

- costs of ordering
- costs of storage.

The EOQ principle is illustrated in figure 3.1, although you should note that the formula that follows afterwards is much more commonly used to calculate EOQ: the diagram merely illustrates the principle.

Figure 3.1: The EOQ principle

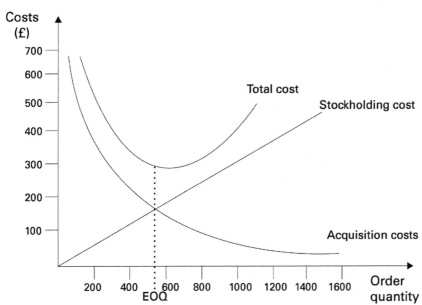

EOQ may be calculated by the following formula (although you should note that, if you read about this, you may find other formulae in various texts), assuming that usage is steady, price per unit does not alter with quantity, and storage costs and purchase order costs are fairly static:

3

$$EOQ = \sqrt{\frac{200\,Ax}{y}}$$

where A = total annual consumption (in pounds), x = cost of issuing order (in pounds), and y = cost per annum of holding stock (as a percentage of the item's average stock value; usually between 20% and 30%).

To calculate an economic order quantity, the following information should be known:

1   usage rate per annum
2   cost per unit
3   cost of placing order
4   cost per annum of holding stock.

Suppose examination of the stock records for a commodity yields this information:

(1) = 1,000, (2) = £1 each, (3) = £0.5 and (4) = 20% (0.2). Then:

$$EOQ = \sqrt{\frac{200 \times 1,000 \times 0.5}{0.2}} = \sqrt{\frac{200 \times 500}{0.2}} = \sqrt{500,000} = 707.1$$

In practice, 700 would be ordered every eight months or so.

EOQ limitations

There are several factors that may limit the usefulness of the EOQ theory, including:

- It does not consider discounts or price breaks.
- There are usually fixed elements in order or storage costs, so that these will not vary directly with the number of orders placed or volume of stock held.
- Storage space may be limited.
- It assumes constant demand.
- It assumes constant lead time.
- Cost information is based on estimates and may not, therefore, give an accurate EOQ figure.
- It does not take account of shelf-life.
- It takes no account of transport features such as load sizes, packaging requirements and journey distance.

Learning activity 3.3

Does your organisation use the EOQ formula? If so, note down how it compensates for some of the limitations. If your organisation does not use EOQ try to find out why not.

Feedback on page 33

Now attempt this:

3

Self-assessment question 3.3

Calculate the EOQ given the following data:

- annual usage = 10,000
- cost of item = £150.00
- ordering cost = £40.00
- cost of stockholding = 25% (of the unit value).

Use the data you have calculated to write a report on EOQ, illustrating its drawbacks.

Feedback on page 33

3.4 Stock replenishment systems including the calculation of reorder points and buffer (or 'insurance') stocks (also known as 'safety stock')

There are two major types of stock replenishment system that are in general use. These are:

- reorder point systems
- scheduling systems.

We shall examine both concepts and consider their strengths and weaknesses.

Reorder point systems

The logic of a reorder point system is to trigger the reordering process every time the inventory level of an item falls to a predetermined level. It is a simple concept, which is why many organisations use it and lends itself well to computer-based stock control systems.

Figure 3.2, often known as the 'sawtooth' diagram, shows how a reorder level system works.

Figure 3.2: Reorder point systems

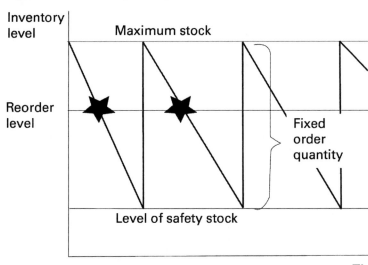

It shows an 'ideal' situation in which the depletion of stock is at quite a constant rate, with the next delivery occurring at the safety stock level. In reality, issues from stock are often irregular, with periods when no stock is issued and others with above average issues.

The reorder level is calculated by adding the best estimate of average demand in the lead time to the safety stock quantity:

Reorder level = Average usage in the lead time + Required level of safety stock

Learning activity 3.4

Given the following data, what should the reorder level be?

- buffer stock = 100
- supply lead time = 6 weeks
- average weekly demand = 200.

Feedback on page 34

Scheduling system

For many organisations, reordering of supplies takes place at fixed cycles (that is, weekly or monthly), illustrated by figure 3.3.

Figure 3.3: A scheduling (fixed interval, variable quantity) stock replenishment system

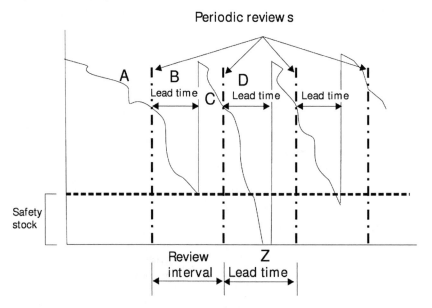

At the review point the decision of how much to reorder needs to be made. When ordering at point A in the diagram, it is necessary to order a quantity that should ensure that there is sufficient stock to cover issues until point D. The next review does not occur until point C and although at this point a larger order is placed, it is too late to avoid running out of stock at point Z.

On average the amount ordered will be equal to the quantity used in the review interval.

The formula to calculate the actual order size at the review point needs to take account of actual physical stock plus what is already on order but not yet delivered together with planned safety stock and expected demand.

The formula to calculate order size is:

Order size = (Demand over lead time + demand over review interval) + safety stock - physical stock - stock on order.

Calculation of buffer stocks

Buffer stocks are needed to protect the organisation against supply problems or delays or against fluctuating lead times, particularly for important items.

There are many computer-based models that will calculate these, but the essential fact is that buffer stocks may be calculated based on usage of the item during the lead time. Thus, if the lead time is 2 weeks and usage is 100 per week, the amount of buffer stock should be 200. The only problem with this occurs if the lead time of an item varies considerably because, if the lead time on one occasion is 2 weeks and then is 4 weeks the next time and 1 week the time after, it is virtually impossible to calculate a buffer stock. Computer-based models will be able to calculate the probability of what the lead time is likely to be, and if the desired service level is added, a buffer stock quantity can be calculated.

Self-assessment question 3.4

Figure 3.4: A scheduling (fixed interval, variable quantity) stock replenishment system

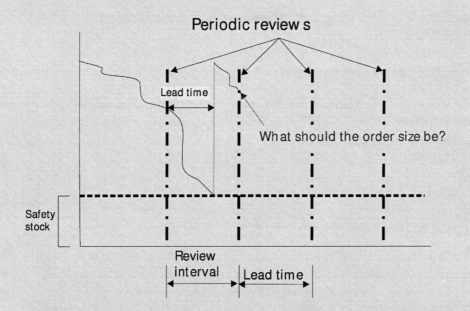

Using figure 3.4 as a reference and given the following data, what quantity should be reordered?

(continued on next page)

3

Self-assessment question 3.4 *(continued)*

Demand per week = 100

Lead time = 3 weeks

Review interval = 4 weeks

Safety stock = 300

Physical stock = 200

On order = 450

Feedback on page 34

Revision question

Now try the revision question for this session on page 195.

Summary

In this study session we have focused on issues surrounding the right quantity including:

- How to determine the right quantity including demand considerations.
- The reasons for suppliers' MOQ and how to counteract them.
- EOQ, how to calculate it and its limitations.
- The nature and uses of FOP and cyclical provisioning.

Suggested further reading

You might like to read more about this topic in sections 10.9–10.15 of Lysons and Farrington (2006).

Feedback on learning activities and self-assessment questions

Feedback on learning activity 3.1

There is no specific feedback because of the individual nature of the activity. However, you should have been able to identify a formal approach to determining and/or calculating the quantity to be ordered in your organisation.

Feedback on self-assessment question 3.1

First, you need to indicate the type of organisation you are discussing.

- In a manufacturing company quantities should be based on forecasted production quantities, which will, in turn, be based on forecasted sales demand for the company's finished product.
- In a retail company quantities of materials should be those that match the stock planning and control system. Give yourself extra credit if you mentioned EPOS.

- Give yourself extra credit if you discussed possible suppliers' influence on purchased quantities, arising out of, for example, bulk discounts.

Feedback on learning activity 3.2

You may have found that the answer is that not much can be done. The text may have provided some options that you could consider.

Feedback on self-assessment question 3.2

Buying items affected by MOQ is likely to result in increased stock levels, which, in turn, leads to higher storage costs, something you are anxious to avoid. The costs likely to be incurred are:

- The cost of financing the stock: that is, the interest paid if the stock is financed from the company's overdraft facility.
- Cost of wastage, for example through theft, damage or obsolescence.
- Cost of personnel to manage the warehouse. Higher stock levels might require additional personnel.
- Cost of providing the stores building. Higher stock levels might require additional buildings or an extension to the existing one.
- Cost of rent and rates on the possible larger building as well as the increased costs of energy consumption and water.

You need to develop these into an argument that might convince the manager to change the requirement.

Feedback on learning activity 3.3

There is no specific feedback because much depends on the nature of the organisation and whether or not it uses EOQ. If, for example, storage space is limited, your organisation might negotiate that deliveries are made in line with storage availability. As an example, if the EOQ was 500 delivered twice a year but there was only space for 250, the purchaser might order 500 every 6 months but request deliveries of 250 every 3 months.

If the organisation does not use EOQ, the reasons are likely to be similar to those expressed in the text.

Feedback on self-assessment question 3.3

Your calculation should give an EOQ of 1460.5934. Obviously, you cannot order 1460.5934 items, and so you would round it to the nearest 'sensible' number, for example 1460. If there were a price break at 1500, you might use the formula as a guide only and order 1500.

This kind of 'approximation' might be one of the first drawbacks you consider. Others might be:

- It does not consider discounts or price breaks.
- There are usually fixed elements in order or storage costs, so that these will not vary directly with the number of orders placed or volume of stock held.

3

- Storage space may be strictly limited.
- It assumes constant demand.
- It assumes constant lead time.
- Cost information is based on estimates, and may not therefore give an accurate EOQ figure.
- The formula does not take account of shelf-life.
- The formula takes no account of transport features such as load sizes, packaging requirements or journey distance.

You may not have mentioned all of these but you should try to give details of those that you do mention. For example if you say that the formula does not take account of shelf-life, you should say that the quantity provided by the formula, if ordered, might lead to some deterioration before the items are all used.

Feedback on learning activity 3.4

You should have calculated that the reorder level = 1300, derived from the average usage in a lead time being 200 × 6 = 1200 + 100 (buffer stock).

Feedback on self-assessment question 3.4

Order size = demand over lead time + demand over review interval + safety stock − physical stock − stock on order. Thus:

Order size = 300 + 400 + 300 - 200 - 450 (= 350).

Ensuring delivery to the right place

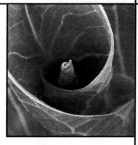

Introduction

In this session we shall address the question of delivery to the right place. To many buyers the idea of having goods delivered to the right place is easy: you just tell the supplier where to deliver them. It is not always as easy as this, however, and issues such as what type of transport to use for deliveries come into play. In this session, therefore, we shall examine the question of how we try to ensure that goods are delivered to the right place, as well as considering what type(s) of transport to use or to suggest/insist that suppliers use. We shall also extend the transport theme into the international arena by considering international transport and its documentation as well as considering packaging.

If goods are not delivered to where you want them, they are not much good. So how do we make sure that they are delivered to where we want them?

Session learning objectives

After completing this session you should be able to:

4.1 State the need to ensure that deliveries are made to the right place, including why this might not happen.
4.2 Identify different transport types and their advantages and disadvantages.
4.3 Describe the selection process for the type(s) of transport to use.
4.4 Explain how to ensure that appropriate transport documentation is available.
4.5 Describe the different types of packaging available and their uses.

Unit content coverage

This study session covers the following topics from the official CIPS unit content document:

Learning outcome

Discuss the importance of the best practice relating to setting objectives within purchasing.

Learning objective

1.4 Right place – inbound transportation of goods to the delivery point, issues arising from UK and international transportation including:
- Selecting transport types
- Ensuring availability of appropriate documentation
- Types of packaging

4

Prior knowledge

None although previous sessions might 'set the scene' to some extent.

Resources

None specific, although a good understanding of what type of transport (and related issues) is the norm at your place of work would be useful.

Timing

You should set aside about 3½ hours to read and complete this session, including learning activities, self-assessment questions, the suggested further reading (if any) and the revision question.

4.1 Ensuring that deliveries are made to the right place, why it is important, and why it might not happen in practice

Why do so many deliveries go astray? How do we prevent misplaced deliveries from happening?

First, every purchase order should define delivery requirements, including the responsibilities and liabilities associated with getting goods from the supplier's premises to the required delivery point. The following points need to be considered:

- The precise delivery point (full postal address).
- Contact person at the delivery address.
- Constraints to delivery:
    - restrictions on size and/or weight of delivery vehicle and packages that can be accommodated
    - times when delivery cannot be accepted, particularly important with the increasing use of delivery 'windows' by many organisations.
- Type and cost of transport (see sections 4.2 and 4.3 below).
- Administration cost of managing the transportation.
- Responsibility and liability for loss or damage sustained during transport/insurance of goods during transit. Buyers will usually stipulate that the supplier would be liable for this.

If a supplier's products are needed at many locations, it may be most cost-effective to have the supplier deliver a single bulk shipment to a central store and the buyer to take responsibility for shipping the individual requirements onward. Alternatively, the supplier can be instructed to make several smaller shipments to the different locations. Each option should be assessed in terms of:

- the risk associated with getting the goods, undamaged, to their final destination when required
- the cost.

What if goods are not delivered to the right place?

Consequences of this could include:

- Delay in correct delivery of the goods, leading to a temporary halt to your organisation's operations, with attendant cost consequences.
- Cost of locating the goods and bringing them to where they should be, and even if the supplier does this, if they are at fault, there is still the cost of potential delays.

4

Learning activity 4.1

Think about any situations at work where deliveries have been made to the wrong place and how this fact was identified, what problems it caused, and how it was rectified.

Feedback on page 44

How do we find out if deliveries have gone astray?

This often happens only when the user tells you that they have not received the goods they were expecting, which is often too late to avoid some of the costs described above. Sometimes you become aware of wayward deliveries only when the person or organisation that has received them tells you that they have them.

If a proper expediting system is in use, so that the progress of every order is known at all times, buyers should become aware of problems associated with delivery earlier and should then be better able to solve them.

Self-assessment question 4.1

Write a memorandum to your subordinates indicating the details that should be included on a purchase order to try to ensure delivery to the right place.

Feedback on page 44

4.2 Different transport types and their advantages and disadvantages

This section covers road, rail, air and water transport and the advantages and disadvantages of each, assuming that the buyer has a choice of which transport mode should be used for supplies. In practice this choice might be dictated by the supplier, but the buyer's loading and unloading facilities, as well as preferences, should play a part in the decision.

4

Road

Transport in the UK is strongly biased towards road transport. The main advantages are as follows:

- flexibility: many types of vehicle available
- versatility: not constrained by timetables and is usually door to door
- competitiveness (there are many third-party operators)
- well-developed road system with pricing not related to usage (flat-rate tax).

The main disadvantages are:

- waiting time caused by congestion
- pilfering
- adverse weather conditions
- increasing legislative controls.

Increasingly, there is concern about pollution caused by road vehicles.

Rail

Rail transport offers several advantages over road transport:

- high capacity: railways can carry a lot of material, making it particularly suitable for bulk transport
- speed: once the goods are loaded then transport between terminals is fast
- safety and security
- rarely affected by weather conditions.

Hence for large or bulky goods rail can prove an attractive mode. The main disadvantage is its inflexibility; in particular it is not door to door and therefore requires additional handling to and from freight yards.

Air

This is a more recent but rapidly growing method of transport, although in smaller countries such as the UK it is rarely used for internal transport. The advantages of air transport can be summarised as:

- speed
- safety and security
- comprehensive scheduled network
- it is highly suitable for perishable items because of its speed.

There are, however, several disadvantages that require consideration, as the method is not suitable for all goods. These include:

- high cost
- limited capacity (meaning it is mainly suitable for goods with a high value to weight ratio – that is, small, high-value goods)
- subject to delays/susceptible to adverse weather conditions
- cannot be used for dangerous substances/goods

- additional handling to and from airports
- there may be no airport nearby.

Sea and canal

Both sea transport and inland waterways offer similar advantages:

- high capacity
- low unit costs
- versatility.

Consequently they are ideal methods for transporting low-value bulky goods. The main disadvantages are those of slowness and delays due to adverse weather conditions.

The decision as to what type of transport to use will be covered in the next section.

Learning activity 4.2

Think about the type(s) of transport your organisation uses for transporting goods. Do they present any problems? If so, what kind of problem? Could you recommend a better type of transport? If you can, what reasons would you put forward?

Feedback on page 45

Now try this:

Self-assessment question 4.2

Question 1. Which of the following is an advantage of sea transport?

1   speed
2   lack of congestion
3   high capacity
4   versatility

Question 2. Which of the following would be a disadvantage of road transport?

1   It causes pollution.
2   It is slow.
3   There is not a well-developed system.
4   It is constrained by timetables.

Question 3. Which of the following is an advantage of rail transport?

1   It gives door to door delivery.
2   It is more secure than road transport

(continued on next page)

Self-assessment question 4.2 *(continued)*

3 It is versatile.
4 There is a comprehensive scheduled network.

Feedback on page 45

4.3 How to select the type(s) of transport to use

In this section we shall apply knowledge gained in section 4.2 above to practical situations and give an idea as to how to decide what type(s) of transport should be used.

You should be as proactive as possible in determining costs, frequencies, service levels and type(s) of transport used on deliveries of goods inward. Part of these considerations should include the following:

- the value of the product
- the physical characteristics of the product (for example, perishability, shelf-life, ease of damage)
- the costs incurred by the supplier and haulier or logistics company
- the level of competition in the supply market (that is, third-party operators)
- security issues
- operational and administrative ease of dealing with certain suppliers/hauliers.

Learning activity 4.3

Consider the type(s) of transport used where you work for different contracts or different goods being supplied. Record your experiences relating to how the choice of transport was made and compare them with what you have read. Are there any plans to change the type of transport used? When you have read the text, think about whether you would recommend any changes and why.

Feedback on page 45

It is important for an organisation to have a transport strategy for all categories of movement of goods, and the following features need to be considered:

- Lowest possible total cost, calculated over the long term.
- Due attention to safety (of people) and security (of goods).
- Speed: this is almost always important, and in some cases is the most critical factor (for example, in transporting perishable goods or medical supplies).
- Convenience: to manufacturers, wholesalers; distributors, retailers and consumers.
- Flexibility: to cope with different types of goods, and different sizes of consignment.
- Reliability: to ensure operations are not disrupted.

You will need to decide the type of transport considered in section 4.2 that is most appropriate for a given delivery situation assuming there is a choice, of course.

Self-assessment question 4.3

Draft a report about the selection of the most appropriate type of transport for transporting 100 new cars (meaning that it is undesirable to drive them) from London to Glasgow.

Feedback on page 45

4.4 International transport documentation including Incoterms

Documentation for domestic transportation is fairly straightforward, usually just consisting of an advice note and/or a packing note provided by the seller to the buyer. In international dealings, life is much more complicated. Much more can go wrong with international transport, and there is not the close geographical contact, helpful in solving problems, that exists between buyers and suppliers located in the same country.

For international transport, to try to minimise problems at the outset, all buyers and suppliers need to agree who should be responsible for delivering the goods. Guidelines have been developed called **Incoterms** to help buyer and seller avoid misunderstandings about the responsibilities of both parties.

Incoterms

Incoterms benefit both the buyer and the supplier because they define:

- the precise place of delivery from the supplier (place)
- responsibility for costs of freight, carriage and insurance borne by either party (costs)
- the point at which risk passes from seller to buyer (risk).

They also avoid any misunderstanding about:

- responsibility for customs clearance
- who should pay the costs of loading, transport and final delivery of the goods
- who should bear the risk of loss or damage to the goods in transit
- who should take out insurance insure against these risks.

The details of individual Incoterms are complex, and you will be able to examine them later in your CIPS studies.

Letters of credit

In domestic purchases, once the order is complete, payment is made in accordance with the payment terms agreed within the contract.

4

For international contracts things are not quite so simple. The seller would prefer to be paid before the goods were released, and the buyer would prefer the goods to be received before payment was made.

A letter of credit solves this problem, because it assures the purchaser that the goods will be delivered as specified and therefore allows payment before receipt. How does it work?

The purchaser and seller agree that payment is by letter of credit, and the purchaser will stipulate what documents the seller must present in order to receive payment, including:

- transport documents to prove that the goods have been despatched
- certificate of quality or third-party inspection certificate
- certificate of origin, to establish where the goods originated
- commercial invoice
- insurance certificate.

The purchaser now instructs their bank to send a letter of credit to the supplier's bank, which in turn informs the supplier. The supplier despatches the goods and presents the stipulated documents to their bank. If all is in order the seller is paid.

The advising bank now sends the documents to the issuing bank, which in turn pays the advising bank. The issuing bank claims payment from the purchaser and releases the documents so that the purchaser can claim the goods.

Learning activity 4.4

Find out which Incoterm(s) are used at your place of work and make a note of the reasons for this choice.

Feedback on page 46

Now try the following self-assessment question:

Self-assessment question 4.4

Question 1. Which of the following do Incoterms define?

1   the mode of transport
2   the type of packaging
3   responsibility for customs clearance
4   which transport company to use

Question 2. Which of the following is a document that a seller should present to secure payment in an international contract?

1   advice note
2   commercial invoice

(continued on next page)

Self-assessment question 4.4 *(continued)*

3 goods received note
4 order acknowledgement

Feedback on page 46

4.5 Packaging considerations

The aim of packaging is to ensure that goods arrive in good condition. This is particularly important for international purchases because of the long distances travelled, sometimes with much movement, for example in rough seas, and the amount of loading/unloading that takes place in a typical international journey.

Learning activity 4.5

Think about items that are purchased from overseas where you work. Do any of them arrive damaged or with parts missing? If necessary, talk to other people such as users to find the answers to this question. Could you suggest any improvements to the packaging used by your suppliers?

Feedback on page 46

There is no universal 'correct' type of packaging. Each item and its journey needs to be considered individually, but the goods must withstand:

- natural hazards (heat, cold, damp, etc)
- handling stresses
- frequent changes in transport mode, for example road to rail to sea to road
- they must also be safe against attempted pilferage, and the packaging should prevent damage during the journey.

Buyers must ensure that international suppliers consider all of these things when deciding what type of packaging to use, and they might need to give suppliers specific packaging instructions in some situations.

Self-assessment question 4.5

These are 'true or false' questions:

Question 1. Packaging should prevent pilferage: true or false?

Question 2. The cheapest packaging available should be used: true or false?

Question 3. Packaging might need to withstand many transport mode changes in a journey: true or false?

(continued on next page)

Self-assessment question 4.5 *(continued)*

Question 4. Packaging might need to withstand temperature changes during a journey: true or false?

Feedback on page 46

4

Revision question

Now try the revision question for this session on page 195.

Summary

In this lesson we have considered various aspects of delivery to the right place, including some of the consequences of not ensuring correct delivery, as well as transport considerations such as which mode of transport to use. We have also considered the increasingly important aspect of transport from international suppliers, including an overview of some of the documentation requirements and use of packaging.

Suggested further reading

You will find much more detailed information on the topics contained in this session in chapter 13 of Lysons and Farrington (2006) and in chapter 13 of Baily et al (2004).

Feedback on learning activities and self-assessment questions

Feedback on learning activity 4.1

There is no specific feedback because of the nature of the activity, but typical ways in which wrong deliveries may be identified include:

- the requisitioner making it known that they have not received it
- another company telling you that the item has been delivered to them by mistake.

Problems usually include operations halting due to lack of the item. Reordering at the supplier's expense, if it was their fault, can rectify the problem, as can retrieving it from where it has been delivered.

The activity should have made you think about problems associated with delivery to the wrong place and how you have become aware of such situations.

Feedback on self-assessment question 4.1

Your answer should include:

- full postal address(es), including details such as postcode(s)

- contact person at delivery point
- any specific instructions as to how to find the delivery location if this is likely to present problems
- any delivery constraints (for example, 'windows')
- type of transport required or preferred.

You may have added type of packaging and packaging units.

Feedback on learning activity 4.2

Again, there is no specific feedback, given the nature of the activity. However, problems with transport, where experienced, are likely to be in line with the above text. Thus, for example, a common problem with road transport is congestion, and a common problem with sea transport is slowness. In terms of recommending better transport types, you should realise that transport types are not universally interchangeable. Sea transport is not interchangeable with rail transport, for example, and waterways and rail transport are possible only if your country has viable water and rail networks. Not all countries, by any means, have both, so that, for example, waterway transport is not used greatly in the UK but is much more widely used in continental Europe.

Feedback on self-assessment question 4.2

Question 1: the correct answer is 3.

Question 2: the correct answer is 1.

Question 3: the correct answer is 2.

Feedback on learning activity 4.3

Any specific feedback is impossible, given the nature of the activity. However, you should have thought carefully about transport used in your workplace and become aware of why the choice of type(s) was made. Recommendations that you might suggest for change would depend totally on your work situation but, for example, if you are currently using road transport you might feel that rail transport might be quicker. If you do make such a recommendation remember the time and cost of loading and unloading goods onto railway trucks, because it is rare, although not unknown, for rail transport to be door to door.

Feedback on self-assessment question 4.3

A variety of transport types is possible here. The cars could be transported by road, rail or sea, although air transport is not possible. If road transport were used, several car transporters would be required, which would mean that the cost would be likely to be high. Road transport, however, would be relatively quick.

Rail transport could provide one 'dedicated' train for such a consignment, and there are rail terminals in both London and Glasgow. However, the

4

cars would have to be taken to the London terminal by road, either on transporters or driven themselves, the latter of which would be undesirable and would take time and increase cost. The same would apply in reverse in Glasgow. The actual journey between London and Glasgow, however, would be quick.

Sea transport would be possible. One hundred cars would easily fit into a relatively small ship, and so the cost would not be too high. The problem, as ever, with sea transport would be that it would be slow, and there is a similar loading and unloading problem to that with rail transport.

The choice of transport depends on which is most important given the situation: cost or speed. If cost is important but speed is not so important, sea transport might be the best option. Rail might offer a reasonable compromise despite the problems of getting the cars to and from rail terminals. There is no one definite answer, and you should have highlighted as many of these issues as possible.

Feedback on learning activity 4.4

Again, there is no specific feedback, given the nature of the activity. If your company uses the DDP (delivered duty paid) Incoterm, for example, it is probably because it is seen as being the most convenient because it means that the supplier will deliver the goods to your premises with all duties and freight charges paid. If it uses ex-works (EXW) it might be because it has its own transport fleet operating near the supplier's location, and using this might be cheaper and more convenient than leaving the supplier to arrange transport.

Feedback on self-assessment question 4.4

Question 1: the correct answer is 3.

Question 2: the correct answer is 2.

Feedback on learning activity 4.5

If you find instances of damage, theft and so on, you need to think about stronger packaging. For example, if your company is using cardboard boxes and damage is occurring because of the box becoming damp, consider using wooden boxes. These might be more expensive but if they prevent problems they may be worthwhile.

Feedback on self-assessment question 4.5

Question 1: true.

Question 2: false.

Question 3: true.

Question 4: true.

Ensuring delivery at the right time

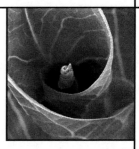

'There is always room for those who can be relied upon to *deliver* the goods when they say they will.'
Napoleon Hill

5

Introduction

In days gone by, buyers were often quite happy for goods to arrive early; in fact some buyers would have said that there is no such thing as too early. Too late – well, that was different! The fact is that both too early and too late are 'bad things'. Let us deal with too late first because it is the more obvious of the two.

If goods arrive too late, there is a risk that your operations will be halted, and this can apply to manufacturing, the provision of a service that is dependent on materials, retailing, or any other kind of operation that needs materials. If operations are halted, even for a short time, the cost can be enormous either in financial terms or, if the delay is serious, in terms of adverse publicity.

If goods arrive too early, they will have to be paid for and kept in stock until they are required. This will involve unnecessary storage costs. Also, there is a risk that the goods might deteriorate before they are used, leading to costs of replacement.

Session learning objectives

After completing this session you should be able to:

5.1 Identify differences between types of lead time (internal, external, total).
5.2 Identify the factors that might influence lead time.
5.3 Describe the process of expediting, including its importance.
5.4 Describe how to measure supplier delivery performance.
5.5 Describe logistics operators' systems.

Unit content coverage

This study session covers the following topics from the official CIPS unit content document:

Learning outcome

Discuss the importance of the best practice relating to setting objectives within purchasing.

Learning objective

1.5 Right time – internal, external and total lead time and factors that influence lead time, expediting, and measuring supplier delivery performance

- Understanding the real meaning of lead time: origination of need to fulfilment of need
- Demand factors
- The need for buffer stocks
- Minimum stock levels
- Supplier's production times
- Logistics operator's operational systems

Prior knowledge

None although previous sessions might 'set the scene' to some extent.

Resources

None specific although a good knowledge of delivery procedures and likely problems caused by early or late delivery in your workplace would be useful.

Timing

You should set aside about 2¾ hours to read and complete this session, including learning activities, self-assessment questions, the suggested further reading (if any) and the revision question.

5.1 Different types of lead time

There are many definitions of the phrase 'lead time'. None is 'right' or 'wrong', but there are 11 stages in the complete process to which lead time refers:

1 Origin of need.
2 Requisition.
3 Order sent to supplier.
4 Order received by supplier.
5 Supplier's manufacturing process commenced.
6 Manufacture completed.
7 Despatch by supplier.
8 Receipt at buyer's premises.
9 Goods available on buyer's premises.
10 Goods in user's possession.
11 Use or consumption of goods (need satisfied).

Learning activity 5.1

Think about how you would define 'lead time'; with which activity do you think it starts and with which one does it end? Talk to colleagues and find out if they have the same view as you. Note down your answers.

Feedback on page 53

Different ideas on lead time

The term 'lead time' is often used in place of, or alongside, 'delivery'. To add to the confusion, 'lead time' can have different meanings, as follows:

- Internal lead time is the elapsed time between identifying the need for a product or service, and issue of a complete purchase order. This will include preparing the specification, identifying suitable suppliers, the enquiry/quotation process, and finally selecting the supplier and agreeing the contract.
- External lead time is the elapsed time between the supplier receiving the purchase order and completing the purchase order.
- Total lead time is the elapsed time between identifying the need for a product or service and the supplier completing the purchase order satisfactorily. From a purchasing point of view, 'total lead time' is the best one to use because it covers all eventualities. It comprises the following stages (figure 5.1).

Figure 5.1: Different ideas on lead time

Stage	Total or 'true' lead time	User's view of lead time	Purchasing lead time	Seller's lead time	Maker's lead time
1. Origin of need					
2. Requisition					
3. Order sent to supplier					
4. Order received by supplier					
5. Supplier's manufacture commenced					
6. Manufacture completed					
7. Despatch					
8. Receipt at buyer's premises					
9. Goods available on buyer's premises					
10. Goods in user's possession					
11. Use or consumption of goods					

You should see from this that lead time is longer than delivery time, and that delays *may* be attributable to the purchaser. This is certainly true of stages 1, 2, 3, 4, 7 and 8: the purchaser can control these to try to reduce total lead time.

Self-assessment question 5.1

Complete the following:

1 Total lead time is the time between origin of need and ...

(continued on next page)

Self-assessment question 5.1 *(continued)*

2 The stages in total lead time that can be controlled by the purchaser are numbers ...

3 Internal lead time is the time between identification of need and ...

Feedback on page 54

5.2 Further lead time considerations

Internal lead time is often a significant part of total lead time, but is often neglected. Any attempts to reduce lead time should focus on internal as well as external (supplier) lead time because:

- The supplier's lead time may be extended if the buyer has not provided sufficient or accurate information to the supplier.
- Quality inspections carried out by the buyer at the supplier's premises can add to the total lead time although, from a quality viewpoint, they may be useful.
- Lengthy goods inward procedures can add to the total lead time.

Where there are ongoing requirements, the buying organisation can assist the supplier to plan supplies by providing a forecast of how many items will be required on what dates. Where a buyer is unable to give a good forecast, or where demand changes unexpectedly, it is important to select a supplier who is capable of reacting sufficiently quickly.

Learning activity 5.2

Find out, by discussing the issue with other staff if necessary, how lead time is calculated where you work. Check also whether your organisation is able to forecast demand. Note down your findings.

Feedback on page 54

The buyer should make sure that a specific delivery date is agreed with the supplier and clearly stated in the purchase order documentation. Never put 'As soon as possible' as a lead time nor something vague such as '10–14 weeks'.

Suppliers may unscrupulously quote delivery dates that they cannot achieve to win the business. Buyers are responsible for establishing whether quoted dates are realistic. For example, the buyer might establish whether the supplier has the following:

- sufficient available capacity
- credible delivery performance statistics
- sufficient stock of long lead time components
- a good production planning system
- appropriate supply strategies.

Self-assessment question 5.2

Draft a report indicating to subordinates what activities, in what sequence, contribute to total lead time and how the buyer may influence lead time.

Feedback on page 54

5.3 Expediting to ensure delivery times are met

When on-time delivery is important, the buyer may consider it necessary to expedite orders: that is, to ascertain order progress. The buyer may require the supplier to provide a production plan showing when major activities will be completed, against which the expediting will be done. Expediting can be done by telephone, letter, email or visits to the supplier. This last is usually done only for very important and/or complex orders because of its expensive and time-consuming nature.

You should note that expediting is not merely 'chasing' late deliveries; this is too late. It should be done during the lead time of the order as a means of checking that order progress is on schedule. Expediters should use a diary system, either manual or electronic, to tell them which orders require expediting each day.

Learning activity 5.3

Compare the expediting procedures from your workplace with the above text to identify differences and similarities. The aspect you should pay particular attention to is whether expediting is in fact progressing orders to ensure they are on schedule or merely chasing late deliveries and whether a diary system is used.

Feedback on page 54

Now move on to the following self-assessment question.

Self-assessment question 5.3

Draft a report, using workplace systems as a guide if necessary, to explain how you would expedite a major contract for the manufacture and supply of a piece of equipment with a total lead time of 26 weeks and whose timely delivery and installation is critical. Assume the supplier is based in your country.

Feedback on page 54

5

5.4 Measuring supplier delivery performance

When on-time delivery is important, delivery performance will be a key criterion in supplier selection decisions. In such cases, every supplier's delivery performance should be monitored as part of a vendor-rating process to aid future sourcing decisions. It is important to inform suppliers that their delivery performance is being measured, because it often improves when they become aware of this.

Typical delivery performance measures include:

- number or percentage delivered on time
- number or percentage delivered within (say) 5 days of the contractual delivery date
- ratio of average number of days late to agreed contractual delivery time.

As with all statistics, there may be circumstances that need to be taken into account when interpreting them. For example, a delivery may have been made on time, but not booked onto the computer as delivered until several days later. Remember what you will have read in sections 5.1 and 5.2 above about receipt and inspection procedures adding to lead time.

Learning activity 5.4

Think about how supplier delivery performance is measured at your workplace. Are a variety of methods used? Which, if any, appear to be most successful and why? Are the results of any delivery performance measurement used as part of a vendor rating system?

Feedback on page 55

Now try this:

Self-assessment question 5.4

Your organisation is trying to develop a just-in-time (JIT) process. This process would be highly dependent on suppliers supplying goods and materials to strict, repetitive, delivery deadlines.

Write a memorandum on which would be the best method of measurement of existing supplier delivery performance to give an idea of which of your suppliers would be able to support the proposed JIT process.

Feedback on page 55

5.5 Logistics operators' systems

It is likely that most of material that you purchase, irrespective of the sector that you work in, will be delivered by third-party transport operators. Your supplier may have contracted these, or your organisation may use an outsourced transport operator for incoming supplies as well as for transporting goods to customers. It is the incoming supplies that we are most concerned with. Third-party operators can provide many services that give benefit to both buying and selling organisations.

Learning activity 5.5

Access the internet to try to find a summary of the kind of services that large transport operators offer. (Hint: 'Logismarket' might be a good starting point.)

Feedback on page 55

5

Additionally, some operators will look after paperwork requirements for international journeys on behalf of their clients, and many can provide the flexibility to undertake urgent transport requests at short notice. Most operators will also offer sophisticated IT-based route-planning systems to give the most efficient, shortest and quickest journey time.

Many of these services would be prohibitively expensive for in-house provision.

Self-assessment question 5.5

Write a report to your manager outlining whether you think your organisation should outsource transport, giving reasons, whichever way you decide.

Feedback on page 55

Revision question

Now try the revision question for this session on page 195.

Summary

In this session we have considered delivery at the right time, why it is important to a purchaser, and what might happen if it not achieved. We have also considered how suppliers' delivery performance might be monitored, and methods of trying to ensure that delivery deadlines are met by suppliers.

Feedback on learning activities and self-assessment questions

Feedback on learning activity 5.1

There is a range of views as to what constitutes lead time. Read the text that follows and you should get an idea of how a buyer should view the concept of lead time. It may differ from your views or those of your colleagues.

Feedback on self-assessment question 5.1

Question 1: your answer should be 'use or consumption'.

Question 2: your answer should be stages 1, 2, 3, 4, 7 and 8.

Question 3: your answer should be 'issue of a complete purchase order'.

Feedback on learning activity 5.2

Specific feedback is not possible because of the nature of the activity. However, if you have found that your organisation has ongoing requirements that are not forecasted, consider why that might be. For example, is your organisation one that reacts to customer orders that are impossible to forecast? Is it that the market in which your organisation operates is highly volatile, making forecasting difficult?

Feedback on self-assessment question 5.2

The first part of your report relates back to section 5.1 and should include a summary of the following:

1   Preparing the requisition.
2   Sending the requisition to the purchasing department.
3   Processing by the purchasing department from enquiry/quotation to preparation of the order.
4   Sending the order to the supplier.
5   Execution of the order by the supplier.
6   Delivery to the purchaser.
7   Receipt, inspection and storage.
8   Issue to user department.

The second part should contain guidelines such as:

- Provide accurate information to suppliers, where possible.
- Ensure you have suppliers that are capable of matching delivery requirements.
- Try to reduce goods inward and inspection procedures.

Feedback on learning activity 5.3

Many companies, unfortunately, either do not have formal expediting at all or use it merely to chase late orders. You should have identified your organisation's system, if it has one. You should also have identified whether a diary system, either a 'paper' one or computer based, is used or whether expediting is haphazard.

Feedback on self-assessment question 5.3

You should start by explaining that expediting a contract such as this should take place in an organised way, and that you should not wait until the 26 weeks has elapsed before expediting. You should then explain that some form of diary system should be used to contact the supplier on a regular basis during the lead time of the contract. The exact means of contacting the supplier is not important, but the usual methods would be by telephone or email. With a contract such as this, visiting the supplier might be worthwhile.

Feedback on learning activity 5.4

Specific feedback is impossible owing to the nature of the activity. However, you should have identified that a system of measuring late deliveries or of measuring ratios of average late deliveries to agreed delivery date is used. Also, you should have identified whether any such system contributes to vendor rating.

Feedback on self-assessment question 5.4

There is no one 'correct' answer to this question; any of the systems described in the text would suffice. However, owing to the criticality of good delivery performance for JIT, the best method might be to measure any late deliveries against the required delivery time to give an absolute measure of any lateness. You should mention that any delays caused by the purchaser should be identified, and not counted towards the measurement of the suppliers.

Feedback on learning activity 5.5

You should have found that transport operators offer a variety of systems such as:

- Warehousing.
- Groupage: putting several small loads together to make one large load so as to be more economical for the customer.
- Satellite tracking: being able to know where a vehicle is at any given moment so that up-to-date delivery information is always available to customers. With some operators, customers can access this online. Such a system is often considered too expensive for in-house providers.
- Palletisation.
- A variety of different vehicles for different types of load or journey.

Feedback on self-assessment question 5.5

You might not necessarily decide that outsourcing transport is best for your organisation, although most companies in the UK currently outsource transport. Outsourcing does have its problems, such as:

- Perceived lack of control because the drivers are not directly supervised by the purchaser's management.
- Lack of company identity for the purchaser, although you can pay for your company logo to appear on the operator's vehicles.

That said, we have outlined the advantages in the text, and you should have taken these into consideration.

5

Obtaining the right price

'Price is what you pay; value is what you get.'
Warren Buffet

6

Introduction

The 'right' price is one of the 'five rights' of purchasing but is one that is sometimes given undue attention because many people seem to think that the whole job of purchasing involves paying the lowest possible price for materials, and the lowest price is obviously the 'right' price, isn't it? Although this is not really true, because there are many other aspects of a purchase that need to be taken into account, such as quality, delivery at the right time and to the right place and quantity, the 'right' price is still very important. But what is the 'right' price? What does it depend on?

Session learning objectives

After completing this session you should be able to:

6.1 Explain the importance of paying the right price.
6.2 Identify different types of cost and explain their impact on the right price, including such issues as cost building as well as types of cost such as materials, labour, etc.
6.3 Identify the factors affecting how a supplier prices its products or services.

Unit content coverage

This study session covers the following topics from the official CIPS unit content document:

Learning outcome

Right price – discuss the importance of the best practice relating to setting objectives within purchasing.

Learning objective

1.6 Determining the right price including different types of costs and their relationship to the purchase price, including:
• Pricing strategies: skimming, market penetration, psychological
• The concept of cost building
• The elements of cost: materials, labour, overheads, marketing, logistics and profit
• Maintaining profit margins.

6

Prior knowledge

None although previous sessions might 'set the scene' to some extent.

Resources

None specific although a working knowledge of how you determine whether or not a price is right in your workplace would be helpful.

Timing

You should set aside about 2¼ hours to read and complete this session, including learning activities, self-assessment questions, the suggested further reading (if any) and the revision question.

6.1 The importance of paying the right price

Definition of the right price

There could be many, but a good one is 'paying the lowest price possible consistent with quality and service'.

This introduces the idea of 'not paying too much'. Most people, whether in their private lives or in a business context, will not willingly pay more than they need to.

Learning activity 6.1

Think about problems that might arise if a price that is too low is paid. Try to think of real situations from your workplace experience.

Feedback on page 63

Total acquisition cost

Many buyers are tempted to try to pay as little as possible (or as little as they can 'get away with'). There is nothing intrinsically wrong with this approach, but you *must* remember that reducing the price paid might result in problems of quality and/or service because there is often a 'trade-off' between price on the one hand and quality and/or service on the other. Quality is almost always a function of price and service (delivery) might well be, particularly if you want the extra levels of service often demanded by buyers today, such as JIT and/or consignment stocking.

What buyers should perhaps concentrate on is '**total acquisition cost**': in other words, the total cost of ensuring that the right goods of the right quality arrive at the buyer's premises at the right time in the right quantity. The lowest total acquisition cost taking account of quality and service could be described as 'best value'. Total acquisition cost is the price plus the following:

- Discounts or surcharges.
- Exchange rate losses (foreign purchases).
- Cost of storage (if the supplier insists on supplying infrequently in large quantities rather than on a JIT basis or supplies too early: see session 5).
- Cost of inspection (a supplier whose overall quality level is better than another's will require less inspection applied to their goods, thus costing the buyer less in the long run).
- Cost of additional work (a supplier who appears to be asking a very low price might be doing so because their product is only part-finished and may require extra machining, for example).
- Transport cost (including insurance).
- Installation cost (for large pieces of equipment).
- Cost of packaging.

Some of these may be included in the purchase price. However, when you compare quotations, you need to be aware of which quotation includes what so as to make realistic comparisons.

Self-assessment question 6.1

Write a brief memorandum (150 words maximum) to subordinates indicating the difference(s) between price and value and suggest some ways of ensuring that best value is achieved.

Feedback on page 64

6.2 Types of cost incurred by suppliers and their impact on price

The supplier's price

It is important to distinguish between a supplier's costs and the purchase price. The supplier's cost is the cost of providing the product or service. This will include the cost of materials, labour, and an allowance for overheads (rent/rates, heating, lighting and so on). Adding the supplier's profit margin to this gives the purchase price. This is summarised in figure 6.1.

Figure 6.1: Supplier price make-up

Various factors affect a supplier's approach to pricing decisions. The main ones are:

- Cost of production including materials and labour, plus an allocation of overheads.
- The degree of certainty of what is required. A supplier will want to make provision in the price for any unforeseen costs. Such costs are likely to be greater if there is uncertainty over what is required.
- The extent of competition. If the supplier has little or no competition, their prices are likely to be high.
- Market conditions. If demand exceeds the available supply market capacity, prices will rise; if supply exceeds demand, prices will fall.
- Customer perceived value. The supplier will charge a premium price if the customer is known to value the features of the product or service.
- How attractive the customer's business is to the supplier. For example, the supplier will price high if the customer's purchases are low value, are infrequent, and the customer always pays late. The supplier will price lower if the customer represents potentially significant sales growth, or has a reputation for prompt payment, or is a prestigious 'blue chip' purchaser such as Marks and Spencer or Microsoft.

Understanding how suppliers make up their prices helps the buyer to evaluate quoted prices and establish whether they represent good value for money.

The last comment to make is that if a price that is too high – higher than it need be – is paid, either your company's profit is likely to fall or it will have to raise its prices to maintain its profit margin, possibly resulting in a decrease in sales.

Learning activity 6.2

Think about your workplace. Do you have a system for assessing suppliers' costs? If so, what is it and how does it work? If not, do you compare the prices offered by different suppliers for the same item or material? Do you consider any other costs not mentioned in the text?

Feedback on page 64

Now attempt this:

Self-assessment question 6.2

Table 6.1 gives the cost breakdown for four suppliers who you have asked to quote for the annual supply of gearboxes for the forklift trucks that your company manufactures.

(continued on next page)

Self-assessment question 6.2 (continued)

Your boss wants a quick summary of what the suppliers offer and your recommendation.

Table 6.1 Gearbox supplier details

Supplier	Anglia Gearboxes	Britannic Gearboxes	ChinaGears	Gearbox Deutschland
Origin	UK	UK	China	Germany
Market position	Used by competitor manufacturer. Very responsive supplier but big question marks over quality. Recently taken over by a US firm.	Current supplier. Delivery reliability has been very patchy recently leading to several assembly line shutdowns.	New entrant to market: trade reports state that quality is very good.	Highly regarded brand with excellent reputation for long life of product and good customer support.
Raw material and component costs	£325	£300	£250	£385
Labour	£480	£510	£190	£420
Overheads	£120	£160	£100	£190
Transport	£20	£25	£175	£70
Total cost	£945	£995	£715	£1,065
Quoted price	£1,040	£1,145	£737	£1,150

Feedback on page 64

6.3 Factors that might affect how a supplier prices its products or services

In section 6.2 above you will have seen that suppliers' prices are made up of the costs of production of the goods or provision of the service plus profit. Unfortunately, things are not always that simple because suppliers sometimes apply pricing policies for various reasons, and these can 'skew' prices calculated by the above method. It is useful for you to try to be aware of whether a supplier is applying a certain policy because, if you are, you may be able to take action to avoid the effects of such a policy.

Types of pricing policy and what you can do about them

- **Short-term profit maximisation** or '**skimming**'. This is usually when a product is new and has few, if any, competitors. Here a seller will be keen to recoup design and development costs as quickly as possible and, because of lack of competition, will feel safe in charging a high price. If you need the item now you are forced to pay it. However, if you can delay the purchase it may be that, after a time, the seller will be forced, by competitive pressure, to reduce the price.
- **Market penetration**. This is when a seller wants to gain a certain market share within a certain time period. To achieve this, the seller may sell at a low price (one that significantly reduces its profit margin) to attract people to buy the product. Paying a low price may be seen as advantageous, but it will not last, and once the seller has achieved the desired market share, the price is likely to increase.

6

- The '**loss leader**'. This is a policy favoured by many supermarkets, whereby a product is offered at a very low price to attract customers. The hope of the seller is that, having been attracted by the low-priced item, customers will buy many other products that will give the seller a good profit.
- '**Peak**' and '**off-peak**' **pricing**. This is used in areas such as transport and energy. Low prices are offered at times of low demand in an attempt to spread activity more evenly, thus using labour and equipment more effectively. From a buyer's viewpoint, if purchases can be timed to suit the periods of low demand, low prices may be paid, and if this is possible, fine!
- **Contribution pricing**. This is a price aimed at covering operating costs during difficult times rather than making a profit. It is done to avoid shutdown or laying off staff until conditions improve. You can take advantage of such a low price, but remember that the price will almost certainly rise when conditions improve, and beware that the supplier does not cut costs at the expense of quality.

Profit

You should remember that all companies in economies that are not centrally planned need to make a profit, otherwise they will not survive. The issue is to try to ensure that suppliers make a 'fair' profit. What is 'fair' depends on such issues as the supplier's situation and position in the market, as well as on general economic conditions. You should always try to be aware of your suppliers' profit margins, and, if you believe them to be excessive, try to negotiate them down, although this is often difficult unless there is much competition in the market.

Learning activity 6.3

Try to think of situations in your own experience where it has been obvious that a supplier has been applying a pricing policy of some sort. Which policy was it? How did you spot it and what did you do about it?

Feedback on page 65

Now continue to follow the fortunes of the forklift truck manufacturer from the previous section.

Self-assessment question 6.3

The forklift truck manufacturing company for which you work decided to get its supplies of gearboxes from ChinaGears based on the cost analysis from self-assessment question 6.2 above. The gearboxes have proved to be of good quality and the supply has been very reliable.

Two years have passed.

(continued on next page)

Self-assessment question 6.3 *(continued)*

Table 6.2 shows the current prices of the four suppliers from whom you had quotes previously.

Table 6.2 Current gearbox process

Supplier	Anglia Gearboxes	Britanic Gearboxes	ChinaGears	Gearbox Deutschland
Origin	UK	UK	China	Germany
Original price	£1,040	£1,145	£737	£1,150
Current price	£990	£1,145	£880	£1,130

Based on this information:

1   What do you think was the initial pricing policy adopted by ChinaGears?
2   What effect could this have upon your company?
3   What action(s) could you recommend to deal with this situation?

Feedback on page 65

6

Revision question

Now try the revision question for this session on page 196.

Summary

In this session we have considered various aspects of price with a view to providing you with some considerations on how you can ensure you pay the 'right' price. This has involved looking at how suppliers' prices are made up and any pricing policies they might apply.

Suggested further reading

You can read more about this subject in chapter 12 of Lysons and Farrington (2006).

Feedback on learning activities and self-assessment questions

Feedback on learning activity 6.1

Essentially, the main potential problem with paying a price that is too low is that either quality or service or both will suffer. You may have been able to think of examples of this from your workplace and how you dealt with them.

A good starting point is always to be suspicious of prices that seem lower than they should be. If something seems too good to be true, it probably is! The result of paying too low a price is that the buyer pays what is called a total acquisition cost that is too high.

The text that follows explains this further.

Feedback on self-assessment question 6.1

You should have identified that price is simply the money paid to a supplier whereas value is lowest total acquisition cost, taking account of quality and service. There are many ways of ensuring best value, but a starting point is to try to ensure, by supplier appraisal or careful comparison and evaluation of quotations, that a supplier asking a low price will be able to give good quality and service. You could also introduce some of the considerations mentioned in the text, such as inspection costs, transport costs and so on.

Feedback on learning activity 6.2

You should have identified that your organisation has a system for assessing suppliers' costs. If it does not, it is asking for trouble!

Systems vary, but it is likely that you would carefully compare and evaluate detailed quotations and buy from the cheapest pre-qualified supplier. This is the system of quotation comparison, but you might request, at the enquiry stage, that suppliers submit cost breakdowns with their quotations. You might have identified that relevant personnel such as users, designers and operations staff would carefully estimate what an item should cost and compare this against suppliers' asking prices.

Feedback on self-assessment question 6.2

You might have made the following observations:

Britannic Gearboxes. Our current supplier is almost the most expensive and its profit margin at 15% is considerably above the norm. Are we being ripped off? We have not been happy with their reliability as suppliers recently. Therefore we should definitely consider changing suppliers.

ChinaGears. Their price is over one third less than that of Britannic Gearboxes, and this would significantly help to reduce our costs and improve our competitiveness. However, there are issues to consider. How can we be sure of the quality and reliability of supply? Their profit margin is only 3%. Is this sustainable in the future? There are other costs to consider, such as protecting against adverse currency movements. Despite these issues, they must be worth considering.

GearBox Deutschland. There is no doubt that we would get a better gearbox for about the same price as our current supplier. By using this supplier we could help differentiate ourselves on quality and reliability without incurring a significant cost penalty in comparison with the current situation.

Anglia Gearboxes. Some price advantage over current supplier, and profit margin is quite high, so possibly some room for negotiation. However, there are issues over quality, and will the recent takeover cause problems? Might be better to wait and see.

Recommendation:

This depends on the company's strategy: if it is to compete on price, ChinaGears must be a very serious option. If it is to compete on quality, then GearBox Deutschland should be the choice.

You will see that we pick up on some of these issues in the next section.

Feedback on learning activity 6.3

If you have been able to think of such an example it is likely to have been one of those in the text. Possible effects could be that you were able to use it to your advantage if it was a contribution policy or that, if it was a skimming policy, you had to either put up with paying a high price in the short term or consider waiting.

Feedback on self-assessment question 6.3

1   As a new entrant into the market, it looks clear that ChinaGears was adopting a penetration pricing strategy to build up market share. Your company has been captured in this way.
2   The effect on the company is, of course, to reduce its competitive advantage based on price. However, as the figures show, the price offered by ChinaGears is still less than its competitors. So, at this stage, there would be no obvious price advantage in changing suppliers, especially as ChinaGears has performed well.
3   Unless you are a very significant customer of ChinaGears and can use this as leverage, there is not a great deal that you can do other than raise the issue with them and make them aware of your concerns and unhappiness. You could point out that you are keeping a close eye on the price of other suppliers and that you note that in general prices are falling and not going up. (This could, of course, be a welcome reaction from other suppliers driving down their costs and reducing their profit margins in response to the aggressive entry of ChinaGears into the market.)

6

6

The purpose and importance of specifications

Introduction

Specifications are used widely in every type of enterprise, whether private sector or public sector, manufacturing or service. They inform everyone who needs to know what an item is and what it is intended to do; and they play a central role in the achievement of good quality. Many people would say that without good specifications it would be impossible to achieve good quality. They do this by providing a detailed description of the item as well as describing its intended performance including any performance parameters that might exist. Specifications can also be applied to services because a service activity needs to be described in detail just as much as a tangible item does.

Design is not for philosophy – it's for life.
Issey Miyake

7

Session learning objectives

After completing this session you should be able to:

7.1 Explain the meaning of specifications and tolerances.
7.2 Explain the importance and purpose of developing specifications for products.
7.3 Describe how developing specifications for services differs from developing specifications for products.
7.4 Explain the need for the buyer to 'drive' the spec. and the legal aspects of letting the supplier 'drive' the specification.
7.5 Explain the need to ensure that suppliers demonstrate the methodology in delivering products or services and the role of specs. in achieving this goal.

Unit content coverage

This study session covers the following topics from the official CIPS unit content document:

Learning outcome

Contribute towards preparing supplier specifications.

Explain policy and information requirements of the organisation when preparing specifications.

Learning objective

2 Contribute towards the development of specifications.
2.1 Explain the meaning of specifications and tolerances.
  • The definition of a specification
  • Why it is regarded as the heart of the contract

- What are the implications of zero defects
- The need for the buyer to drive the specification
- The legal aspects of letting the supplier drive the specification

Resources

Nothing specific but a good working knowledge of specifications used in your workplace would be useful.

Timing

You should set aside about 3¼ hours to read and complete this session, including learning activities, self-assessment questions, the suggested further reading (if any) and the revision question.

7.1 The meaning of specifications and tolerances

Specifications

A specification can be defined as a statement of requirements to be satisfied by the supply of a product or service. Specifications are a means of communicating to a supplier precisely what is required, so that the products or services supplied meet the needs of the purchasing organisation. Specifications can also be used as a means of assessing what was actually supplied. Specifications do not just refer to the product or service, but include all aspects covered under the 'five rights' such as place of delivery, quantity, and so on.

Specifications form part of the contract between buyer and seller. Contracts are covered in study sessions 17 and 18 of this unit.

Tolerances

When specifying something it is usual to allow some leeway in terms of matching the specification because it is usually impossible to match the requirements *exactly*. This 'leeway' is known as a 'tolerance'. In engineering specifications tolerances are usually extremely small so that, for example, a dimension of 1,000mm *might* have a tolerance of plus or minus (usually expressed as +/−) 1mm. This means that precise measurement would allow any actual dimension between 999mm and 1001mm. In precision engineering terms, such a tolerance would be regarded as extremely generous.

You should be aware that, generally, the tighter the tolerance required, the more expensive it will be to achieve because of the more skilled work required, more time, and the greater likelihood of scrap being produced.

Learning activity 7.1

Find out what type(s) of specification are used where you work. Discuss this with other staff if necessary. Do they convey the kind of information

(continued on next page)

Learning activity 7.1 *(continued)*

mentioned above? How tight would you say any tolerances used are? Write down the salient points of your findings.

Feedback on page 74

Now attempt this:

Self-assessment question 7.1

Write a report to your colleagues explaining the basic purpose of specifications and what their content should be.

Feedback on page 74

7

7.2 The importance and purpose of developing specifications for products

This section includes such issues as letting the supplier know the buyer is in control and giving a definition of requirements, including the removal of any doubt about the requirement.

When buying products it is important that you receive exactly what you require, not a vague approximation of it. Thus, at a simple level, if you want a bucket that will hold 5 litres of water, one that holds only 4.5 litres is no good; in other words, it is not **fit for its purpose**. In more complex engineering environments, requirements are expressed in much more precise terms but the principle is the same: the item must be fit for its purpose.

A product specification achieves this by telling a supplier *exactly* what is required, and if written properly will remove any doubt. Thus, using the example given in section 7.1 above, if a dimension is described as 1,000mm +/– 1mm, the supplier will know that 998mm or less is not acceptable nor is 1002mm or more. Also, if the specification gives precise details of what material(s) the item is made from, the supplier will have no doubt about this issue. There is more room for doubt with service specifications, but if they are written properly, they should tell the service provider exactly what is required as well as when and where and so on.

To achieve this, specifications must be:

- clear and unambiguous
- concise
- comprehensive
- consistent (throughout the specification and with other specifications).

Learning activity 7.2

Think about the specification(s) you use at work and various supply situations. Are there any times when suppliers clearly have been in some doubt as to what you require? If so, was this because of the supplier's

(continued on next page)

7

Learning activity 7.2 *(continued)*

interpretation of the specification or because the specification itself was not precise enough? How was any such situation resolved?

There are many questions here but try to answer them all and write down what you regard as the key points.

Feedback on page 74

Now attempt the following self-assessment question:

Self-assessment question 7.2

Write a memorandum to subordinates explaining the checks that buyers can make regarding specifications before they are passed to suppliers.

Feedback on page 75

7.3 Service specifications

This section will focus particularly on the intangible nature of services and the development of specifications for **services**.

Service specifications have taken on increased significance in recent years, and many organisations have found that it can be very difficult to prepare a good service specification. The result in many cases has been poor service levels or unforeseen costs. Services differ from products in several ways.

- Services are intangible.
- Services involve the performance of activities or tasks.
- Services cannot be owned like a product can.
- Services cannot be stored.
- Samples of services cannot be seen prior to purchase.
- Some services cannot be performed remotely.
- Services are provided by people.

These differences have implications for specifications.

Difficulty in specifying services

Services, being intangible, can be difficult to define. How clean is clean? How long should it take to repair a computer? What is the definition of a good, well-cooked meal? Also, people provide services and people are different. Provision of a standardised service may therefore be difficult. It is also difficult to assess whether the service has been correctly performed. For example, is an architect at fault if the client doesn't like the architect's design?

Specifying when the service is needed

Services cannot be stored, and some services such as catering have to be provided precisely at the time of need. This means that the time of need must be clearly specified so that the service provider can organise the provision of the service efficiently.

Place of service delivery

Many services must be performed at the purchaser's premises, such as catering, security, gardening, and computer maintenance. In this case, several aspects need to be incorporated into the specifications that are unnecessary in a product specification, as follows:

- supervision
- access to premises
- provision of facilities
- confidentiality (the service provider might witness commercially sensitive activities).

Service level agreements

These may form part of the service specification and should not only lay down parameters for supplier performance but should also act as a quantifiable basis by which the supplier can be measured. They will cover such aspects as:

- details of services to be provided
- time and point of service provision
- names of people authorised to provide the service
- required response times, under normal circumstances, and in emergencies
- support and back-up arrangements
- required documentation.

Learning activity 7.3

Imagine you are writing a service specification for office cleaning. Write down the cleanliness standard that you would expect for internal office floors and walls. Use relevant information from your workplace to help you if necessary.

Feedback on page 75

Now attempt this:

Self-assessment question 7.3

Senior managers at your organisation have decided to outsource catering. They have decided simply to bring in a company and 'let them get on with it'. You feel this is the wrong approach, and that a specification for the catering service should be drawn up. Write a report to the management team indicating *why* a specification should be drawn up, and giving some details that it should contain.

Feedback on page 75

7.4 The need for the buyer to 'drive' the specification

The purpose here is to reinforce the material in previous sections that states that a specification should be a description of *what the buyer requires*. This is the meaning of the buyer 'driving' the specification.

A specification should always make it clear that it is describing, in detail, what the buyer requires, and that no substitutes or alternatives will be acceptable without the express agreement of the buyer. This establishes the fact that the buyer is in control of the purchasing process.

Legal considerations of specifications

You should establish whether the product or service must comply with any legislation: for example, CE marking for certain machinery and electrical items destined for European Union countries.

There is much legislation concerning the environment, both nationally and internationally. You should be aware of applicable legislation, and discuss this with the specification team. Examples of products with high environmental risks are given below, and their legislative requirements should be carefully investigated:

- solvents
- degreasants
- chemicals
- herbicides
- gases, such as hydrogen
- pesticides
- oils
- scrap metal.

Another area of increasing legislation is dangerous/hazardous material. The COSHH regulations (Control of Substances Hazardous to Health) and CHIP regulations (Chemicals: Hazard Information and Packaging for Supply) are examples of this.

Although the supplier should be expected to comply with all relevant legislation, the purchasing organisation is still responsible for compliance with the law. Buyers should therefore take a proactive role in communicating known legislative requirements to the supplier.

Learning activity 7.4

Reflect on your reading of the text and précis the salient points to give you a useful aide-mémoire.

Feedback on page 76

Now attempt this:

Self-assessment question 7.4

Think about any legislative requirements that might exist for specifications that you use. Write down areas that might be involved and how you ensure that these requirements are met.

Feedback on page 76

7.5 The importance of the supplier demonstrating the methodology used in delivering products and services

You should always be on the lookout for ways of improving the products or services that you purchase so that you can contribute to the improvement of your organisation's product or service. If you are aware of *how* the supplier produces and delivers products or services, you might be able to identify opportunities for improvement.

It may also be appropriate to get suppliers involved early in the process of determining specifications (a process known as **early supplier involvement** or ESI). This would be the case when the supplier possesses important technical expertise or experience that the buying organisation does not have. The likelihood of arriving at an innovative solution for the specification that reduces cost or lead time, for example, will be significantly improved with the benefit of the supplier's input.

Learning activity 7.5

You may not have encountered such concepts as are discussed above, so try to précis the text to identify the salient points. You might also like to find out whether your organisation uses ESI.

Feedback on page 76

Now try this self-assessment question:

Self-assessment question 7.5

Write a memorandum to subordinates indicating why it is necessary to keep in mind at all times the notion of specification improvement when devising specifications (or at least being involved in the devising process).

Feedback on page 76

Revision question

Now try the revision question for this session on page 196.

Summary

In this session we have considered the nature and purpose of specifications, with emphasis on the role of buyers in their preparation. We have also studied the possible role of suppliers in the preparation and development of specifications.

Suggested further reading

You might like to read about this topic in more detail in chapter 9 of Lysons and Farrington (2006).

Feedback on learning activities and self-assessment questions

Feedback on learning activity 7.1

Specific feedback is impossible because of the nature of the activity. However, your organisation should use some specifications, which might be drawings, technical descriptions or standards. If the specifications are for services, they will probably be fairly 'loose', although they should still describe the activity to be performed. You might think that service specifications do not have tolerances, which you may regard as something that belongs only in engineering. But if you state, for example, that cleaning should start at between 7.00 a.m. and 7.15 a.m., this is a kind of tolerance.

Feedback on self-assessment question 7.1

Your report should include the fact that specifications are:

- a means of communicating requirements to suppliers so that you get what you need
- a means of assessing the quality of products and services.

You should state that all relevant aspects of the 'five rights' should be included so that a specification might tell suppliers what is required, in as much detail as is necessary, when it is required, and where it is required. It might also indicate how the quality of the product would be assessed, and it should provide information about relevant tolerances.

Feedback on learning activity 7.2

Again, specific feedback is impossible because of the nature of the activity but you should focus on any specific reasons for a supplier being in doubt as to what to supply and on how this was resolved. You might have identified, for example, that a specification was changed or rewritten to remove any doubt, or that discussions were held with the supplier to interpret the

7

specification. It could be that specifications in use are not detailed enough, or that situations exist where a supplier that has supplied your organisation for a long time is considered to 'know what is needed' and therefore does not need a specification.

Situations of poor supplier understanding could be resolved by discussions between the supplier and appropriate staff in your organisation.

Feedback on self-assessment question 7.2

It is common for buyers to claim that they cannot play a meaningful role in the development and use of specifications because they are not 'technical'. However, in order to ensure that suppliers fully understand your requirements, you and your subordinates should understand that specifications should be

- clear and unambiguous
- concise
- comprehensive
- consistent (throughout the specification and with other specifications).

Additionally, they should not be over-complex. A good 'rule of thumb' is that, if you do not understand a specification, it is quite likely that your supplier won't either, and such a situation is likely to lead to doubt.

Feedback on learning activity 7.3

There is no *right* answer to this activity, but cleanliness standards for office floors should be something like this:

- Carpeted areas to be visibly free of dirt, litter and grit.
- Hard floors to be visibly free of dirt, dust, stains and spillage.
- All cleaned surfaces shall not be slippery. No mop or other cleaning marks shall be visible.
- Cleanliness standards for internal office walls.
- All walls and wall fitments to be visibly free of dust, dirt and stains.

Feedback on self-assessment question 7.3

The first part ('why') should include the fact that a specification gives a reference point so that the service provision may be measured. Also, it gives the opportunity to include a service level agreement as a further means of measurement. At a more basic level, a specification will tell the service provider exactly what is to be provided, when and where.

There is no 'correct' answer to the question of details but you should include issues such as:

- How many meals are to be provided each day.
- What meals should be provided: is it only lunches, or are breakfasts needed and/or evening meals if shifts are worked?
- What price parameters (for customers) should apply.

- What types of meals should be provided: hot meals, sandwiches and so on.

You may be able to think of other details to include.

Feedback on learning activity 7.4

You should have identified that the salient points are that:

- The buyer should control the specification so that there is no doubt about what is required.
- No alternative should be accepted without agreement.
- The purchaser is legally responsible for ensuring that a specification complies with any relevant legislation.

Feedback on self-assessment question 7.4

Typically such areas will include:

- The recovery, recycling and reusing of materials and waste products.
- The safe disposal of waste products that cannot be recycled.
- Any other that might be relevant to your organisation.

You might ensure that such requirements are met with:

- Supplier selection policies to support firms that conform to environmental standards for air, water and noise pollution.
- Supplier and product selection policies that reflect concern for conservation and the renewal of resources.
- The safe testing of products and materials.

Feedback on learning activity 7.5

You should have identified the following:

- Improving supplied products or services can improve your own organisation's output.
- Knowing how a supplier produces can open up opportunities for suggesting improvements.
- Bringing suppliers in at the design stage (ESI) can yield significant specification improvement.

Feedback on self-assessment question 7.5

You should include the fact that continual improvement in supplied products and services is necessary to improve your own product or service. One way of achieving this is to be aware of how suppliers produce their products or services. Also, if suppliers can contribute at the design stage of your product, they can often develop innovative solutions.

Different types of specification

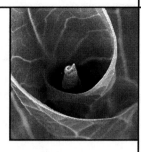

Introduction

This session concerns the use of specifications. Specifications are the way(s) in which you can tell a supplier what they should supply. We shall consider each type, with its advantages and disadvantages, as well as situations in which they should be used. We shall focus particularly on performance specifications, a type of specification we mentioned in study session 2 and one that is used increasingly. We shall also consider the use of standards and the process of standardisation.

What you buy is just about the most important part of the purchasing job. If you do not buy the right product (or service) you might as well not bother! So how do you tell a supplier what they must supply? Read on.

8

Session learning objectives

After completing this session you should be able to:

8.1 Identify the different types of specification.
8.2 Identify the sectors in which each type of specification is used.
8.3 Explain why performance specifications are being used more and more.
8.4 Describe the use of standards.

Unit content coverage

This study session covers the following topics from the official CIPS unit content document:

Learning outcome

Contribute towards preparing supplier specifications.

Explain policy and information requirements of the organisation when preparing specifications.

Learning objective

2 Contributing towards the development of specifications
2.3 Identify the different types of specification and consider the different contexts in which they are used:

Methods	Used in sectors
• Blueprint/design	• Engineering, projects, construction
• Brand name Sample	• Small businesses, consumers
• Market grade	• Textiles, commodities
• Standards	• Commodity trades
• Performance	• Engineering, manufacturing

Methods	Used in sectors
• Chemical/physical • Properties	• Manufacturing, electronics and most sectors • Chemical engineering, engineering, construction

Prior knowledge

Study sessions 2 and 7.

Timing

You should set aside about 2 hours to read and complete this session, including learning activities, self-assessment questions, the suggested further reading (if any) and the revision question.

8.1 Different types of specification in common use

There are many different types of product specification. The buyer should be aware of which type of specification is appropriate for a given requirement, and should discuss this with the person or team preparing the specification.

Learning activity 8.1

Investigate different areas of your organisation and record the types of specification used in the process of purchasing goods and services.

Feedback on page 87

Brand name

These are cheap and easy to write, and should guarantee consistency from one purchase to the next. They may be appropriate for commonly used everyday products and services. A branded product will be more expensive than a non-branded one, although there may be several similar competing brands.

It is usual to add the maker's reference number to the maker's name, so that an example of a brand-name specification for a light bulb might be 'Philips PL * Electronic/C 20'.

Performance specification

Here, the seller is told only the performance that is required, not how to make the item. These specifications are said to contribute to greater supplier commitment to zero defects and continual cost cutting, and are

8

in increasing use in industry. We shall examine them in more detail in section 8.3 below.

Blueprint or engineering drawing

These are commonly used in engineering environments, and have the following advantages:

- They are accurate and precise.
- They are the most practical way of describing mechanical parts requiring close tolerances.
- They allow wide competition, because once the drawing has been produced there is no effective limit to the number of suppliers to whom the drawing can be sent as part of the process of requesting quotations.
- They clearly set the standard for inspection because incoming material can be compared with the drawing to ascertain whether its quality is correct.

The only real drawback to this type of specification is the fact that they tend to be expensive to produce because of the highly qualified, technical personnel required to produce them.

Chemical/physical specification (properties)

These are sometimes known as composition specifications, and refer to the physical or chemical make-up of an item. These specifications are used where safety is important, or when the material is key to performance. For example, using the wrong material could have disastrous consequences when dealing with hazardous products (corrosive chemicals, for example) or extreme temperatures. Their advantage is that they allow testing against the required composition, and their disadvantage is that specialist expertise is required to specify and undertake the testing.

Standards

These are similar to brand names, but they allow wider scope of source of supply, and should be used wherever possible because of simplification. We shall examine them more closely in section 8.4 below.

Samples

A sample can be used to assess the suitability for purpose of an item that *may* be produced if the sample proves satisfactory. The sample should be prepared using the same methods and processes as will be used in the event that an order is placed. Their advantages are:

- They allow the buyer to assess suitability prior to purchase.
- They can be useful where it is difficult to specify the product, as they can give a comparative basis for assessing the performance or suitability of the supplied product.

Their disadvantages are that the purchaser must have some legitimate way of verifying that actual supply is the same as the sample, and the supplier may produce a sample that is of better quality than the actual supply.

8

Technical specification

A technical specification is a highly prescriptive, written specification giving a fully detailed definition of what is required. Such detail may be required where the purchased item must interface with existing plant or systems, or when the purchasing organisation holds greater design expertise. It can include:

- required performance
- physical characteristics (dimensions, strengths, etc)
- design details
- materials
- processes/methods involved in making the product or service
- maintenance requirements
- operational requirements.

The specification should be clear and precise so that the supplier can understand it without any extra interpretation. Its advantages are similar to those of drawings. Its disadvantages are:

- It may involve significant effort to produce.
- The high level of prescription may require the supplier to design a 'one-off', which can add significant cost, when standard items may suffice with little or no modification.
- It may limit the number of suppliers able to comply.
- The risk of the design not resulting in the required performance is borne by the purchaser, because the supplier is simply building to the purchaser's design.

8

Self-assessment question 8.1

Question 1. Which of the following best describes a major disadvantage of technical specifications?

1. The risk of non-performance of the product, when made, is borne by the buyer.
2. It is difficult to verify that the product matches the specification.
3. Too many suppliers might be able to quote for a product specified in this way.
4. They do not provide enough detail for suppliers to produce effectively.

Question 2. Which of the following best describes an advantage of brand-name specifications?

1. The seller is instructed precisely as to the details of manufacture of the product.
2. They are cheap and easy to produce.
3. They allow wide competition.
4. They are the best way of transmitting a high degree of detail such as engineering tolerances.

(continued on next page)

Self-assessment question 8.1 *(continued)*

Question 3. Which of the following specifications describes the physical make-up of a product?

1 Brand name.
2 Standards.
3 Engineering drawings.
4 Composition specifications.

Feedback on page 87

8.2 The sectors in which each type of specification is used

In study session 1 we considered different types of organisation and the essential nature of each of them, as follows:

- manufacturing including 'variations on the theme' such as processing, assembly, etc
- services
- retail
- FMCG
- not-for-profit
- factoring and wholesaling.

In this section we shall consider which type(s) of specification are likely to be used by each type of organisation. As we shall see, the type of specification used depends greatly on the type of product purchased.

Learning activity 8.2

Think about what you would require in terms of a specification for each of the following situations, and record your answers:

1 A major aircraft manufacturer ordering the wing mountings for the jet engines to be fitted to the aircraft.
2 A high street department store stocking electric kettles.
3 A buildings maintenance company outsourcing its cleaning services.
4 A high street bank placing its call centres offshore.

Feedback on page 87

Manufacturing

We can include all of the 'variations' here. In assembly-type operations the main types of specification used for production line components will be **drawings** and **technical specifications**. This is because most of these items will be made especially for a particular purpose, for example a forging used as the counterweight of a forklift truck, and typically will require detailed specification of such matters as engineering tolerances. Also, each item will have to fit together with other components. These types of specification are the best means of transmitting such requirements. In some situations **samples** might be used, although this is not widespread owing to the difficulties mentioned in section 8.1 above.

In process-type industries it is most likely that **composition** specifications would be used.

In both types of organisation, where outsourcing was used, service specifications, which you have seen in study session 7, would be used.

Service organisations

Here, **service specifications** would be used for any specific, specialist outsourced services required as part of the organisation's overall service provision, and the nature of any support materials used for the service provision would mean that **brand name** specifications would be the most likely.

Retail organisations (including FMCG, factoring and wholesale)

The nature of products bought and sold by all of these types of organisation is 'finished goods', and these can be specified by brand name only. The only exceptions would be for any outsourced services, where service specifications would be used, and where 'own brand' products, for example Tesco's cornflakes, were required, a form of composition specification would be used.

'Not-for-profit' organisations

Much of the work carried out by such organisations would require the use of outsourced services, and here service specifications would be used. Any items that, for example, a charity would purchase to be sold, as gifts would be specified by brand name.

Self-assessment question 8.2

Write a brief report outlining what type(s) of specification should be used by (a) a manufacturer and (b) a service provider, giving reasons.

Feedback on page 87

8.3 Why performance specifications are being used more and more

Performance specifications, often known as 'functional specifications', are relatively brief documents (compared with 'conformance' specifications) that define the required function to be achieved, and details of the input parameters; but they do not state how the function should be achieved. It is here that they differ from conformance specifications such as drawings and technical specifications, which usually give the supplier exact details of what materials the item should be produced from, how they should be processed, and so on. Performance specifications may be appropriate where suppliers possess greater design expertise than the purchaser, or where the technology is changing rapidly in the supplying industry. A performance specification can include:

- what is to be achieved (the function)
- the process input
- the operating environment
- details of available utilities (types of energy sources: electricity, gas, and so on)
- interface details
- quality levels
- safety levels
- rules for measuring performance.

When using this type of specification the purchaser is highly reliant on the supplier's expertise, and so it is very important to deal with credible suppliers. We shall examine supplier selection in study sessions 13 – 15. It is also important to understand and communicate to suppliers how their offers will be evaluated, and the criteria for measuring whether the desired function has been achieved. Performance specifications are being used more and more by buyers because they are considered to have the following advantages over conformance specifications.

- Suppliers can use their full expertise and innovation to develop the lowest-cost solution to meet the required performance, quality and safety and so on.
- Less effort is required by the buyer to produce a performance specification compared with a conformance specification.
- The risk of not meeting the required function is borne by the supplier. This can have significant legal implications, meaning that, generally, if a supplier supplies an item to a performance specification and the item does not perform adequately, the buyer will almost certainly have legal redress against the supplier. This is not the case with conformance specifications, where, if the supplier produces to specification and the item does not perform adequately, the buyer will usually have no legal redress.

Performance specifications are said to have the following disadvantages:

- It may be difficult to assess the adequacy of a supplier's quote – that is, that the particular design will work properly. This might be the case where the supplier is using technology that the purchaser is unfamiliar with.
- Comparison of suppliers' offers is lengthy and complex, as each will offer a different solution, making direct comparison difficult.

Learning activity 8.3

Now you know what performance specifications are, note down the type of specifications you use at work. Are they generally performance or

(continued on next page)

Learning activity 8.3 *(continued)*

conformance or a combination of the two? What do you think drives your organisation's choice of specification?

Feedback on page 87

Now:

Self-assessment question 8.3

Draft a report as to why performance specifications might be better than conformance specifications, including an explanation of their objectives.

Feedback on page 88

8.4 Standards and their uses

By 'standards' we mean published standards that define many commonly accepted products, services, safety levels, environmental levels, and so on. Our intention here is to consider the use of standards and their advantages as well as to consider the process of standardisation.

Sources of standards

- Industry standards, for example as developed by trade associations.
- National standards, such as British Standards published by the British Standards Institution (BSI) (UK), some of which may be required by legislation.
- International standards, for example the International Standards Organization (ISO). You may be familiar with the ISO quality standard ISO 9000.

In the EU, progress is being made towards developing standards that will be acceptable as both European and international standards. The European Committee for Standardization (CEN) is doing this.

Features of standards

- Standard terms and symbols, enabling buyers and sellers to speak the same language through the use of standard graphical systems and terminology.
- Dimensional standards, which enable interchangeability of similar parts and rationalisation in range of sizes.
- Definition of adequate standards of performance, quality, and safety.
- Definition of technical requirements, such as tolerances.
- Standard methods of testing.
- Codes of practice to indicate acceptable or recommended methods of use, installation, operation and maintenance.

Buyers should be familiar with the standards that exist for the products and services they purchase, and should identify whether any appropriate standards exist before spending time and money developing an in-house specification.

Advantages of standards

They:

- Simplify comparison of suppliers' quotes if all suppliers quote to the standard.
- Promote competition because suppliers have a common benchmark to quote against.
- Remove uncertainty as to what is required.
- Should mean that the purchaser does not have to write a specification for items covered by standards.

Many standards are complex, and may have the following disadvantages:

- Any standard by its nature is a compromise, agreed by the various parties that prepared it, and it may not satisfy all the purchaser's requirements.
- Standards may not always reflect the latest technology or practices.
- Care needs to be taken when using standards in an international context. For example, British Standards are unlikely to mean much to suppliers in China.

Standardisation

This is closely linked to the use of standards, and involves reaching agreement on such things as size, shape, colour, properties, performance, etc. Organisations frequently purchase a greater variety of products and services than is necessary, often for the following reasons:

- Specifiers prefer to design their own items, and do not establish whether similar items to what they require already exist elsewhere in the organisation.
- The organisation's information systems make it difficult to establish what is already in use.

Lack of standardisation results in increased cost for an organisation, and is generally accentuated in large organisations with multiple sites. The increased costs may be summarised as follows:

- A greater range of items will lead to unnecessary stockholding and handling costs.
- A greater number of small orders will lead to a higher ordering and administrative costs.
- Smaller purchase quantities attract higher prices.

The benefits of standardisation are the opposite of these costs of lack of standardisation. The organisation will be able to aggregate spend into fewer items and negotiate better prices with fewer suppliers. Fewer deliveries will be made, resulting in reduced handling costs. Fewer lines will need to be stocked. The increased volumes and increased interaction with fewer

8

8

suppliers will yield closer communication and understanding between buyer and supplier, and quality levels should improve as a result.

Achieving standardisation is not easy. A standardisation programme should involve all the users of a particular product or service, otherwise there may be resistance to accepting the new standard. Inevitably, some users will have to compromise.

Learning activity 8.4

You should now know something of the nature of standards and the process of standardisation. Think about your organisation. Does it proactively try to use standards where possible? If it does, what benefits does it gain? If it does not, why not?

Have you ever been involved in a standardisation process? If so, what contribution do you believe you were able to make? Note down the salient points.

Feedback on page 88

Now try this:

Self-assessment question 8.4

Compare standards with brand name specifications and describe why there might be problems using standards in an international context.

Feedback on page 88

Revision question

Now try the revision question for this session on page 196.

Summary

In this session we have focused on specifications. These are the ways in which buyers inform suppliers as to what they require, often expressed in a degree of technical detail. You should now be aware of the basic role of specifications and the different types of specification available, and situations in which each type might be used, as well as their respective advantages and disadvantages. You should also be aware of the role of standards and of the principles and purpose of standardisation.

Suggested further reading

You might like to read sections 9.4–9.7 in Lysons and Farrington (2006), in which the aspects we have covered are examined in more detail.

Feedback on learning activities and self-assessment questions

Feedback on learning activity 8.1

There is no specific feedback because of the nature of the activity. Drawings and standards are used in many organisations but, increasingly, performance specifications are used. However, you may have come across a variety of specifications regularly used in your organisation, depending on what is being purchased. The different types of specification in common use follow in the remaining text.

Feedback on self-assessment question 8.1

The correct answer to question 1 is 1.

The correct answer to question 2 is 2.

The correct answer to question 3 is 4.

Feedback on learning activity 8.2

Your answers should come from section 8.1, but you would expect the following:

1   A highly detailed technical specification, possibly supported by drawings.
2   Brand name.
3   A performance specification, perhaps supported by brand names and/or standards for the supporting consumables.
4   A performance specification.

Feedback on self-assessment question 8.2

Typically, a manufacturer would use a combination of drawings, technical specifications and, perhaps, samples for items to be use on the production line and incorporated in the finished product. There may also be some use of brand name specifications if the finished product is assembled from items that are finished products in their own right. Manufacturers would tend to use drawings and technical specifications because of the need for production line components to be manufactured for a particular purpose and made with tight engineering tolerances to be able to fit together with other components and materials.

In service organisations, service specifications are likely to be used for specific parts of the overall service that are outsourced, and support materials are likely to be specified by means of brand name specifications.

Feedback on learning activity 8.3

There is no specific feedback because of the nature of the activity. However, you should have considered the specific advantages and disadvantages

8

of performance specifications and the specific requirements of your organisation. For example, one would expect performance specifications to be used for large, complex pieces of equipment that would be made especially for your organisation, where input of the supplier's expertise would be useful.

Feedback on self-assessment question 8.3

Your report should cover situations where performance specifications would give advantages over conformance specifications, and should include the idea that performance specifications would be useful where the use of suppliers' expertise would be considered essential. You should also give some of the specific advantages of performance specifications, such as:

- Suppliers can use their full expertise and innovation to develop the lowest-cost solution to meet the required performance, quality and safety and so on.
- Less effort is required by the buyer to produce a functional specification compared with a conformance specification.
- The risk of not meeting the required function is borne by the supplier.

Feedback on learning activity 8.4

Again, specific feedback is difficult because of the nature of the activity. However, if your organisation does use standards, the advantages should be in line with those in the text: better competition, easier comparison of quotes, and so on.

If you have been involved in a standardisation process, the kind of contribution you might have made would be to provide information on market standards and suggest where a range of items that was too wide was being purchased.

Feedback on self-assessment question 8.4

Your answer to the first part should revolve around the fact that brand names reduce the available competition because they tie the purchaser to one supplier/manufacturer. Also, brand names tend to be expensive. On the other hand, standards allow wide competition among suppliers and reduce costs because they reduce the number of small orders, attract bulk discounts and reduce stockholding costs.

In an international context standards might present a problem because one country's standard might not mean very much to another country and might not be acceptable in the other country.

The contribution of buyers and sellers to specifications

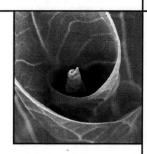

Introduction

In this study session we will consider how buyers and suppliers can contribute to the development of specifications. This is not to suggest that they can usurp what is often seen as the natural role of engineers, designers and users ('technical' people) but buyers can contribute a lot of non-technical information that can assist the specification process and suppliers can use their expertise to make major contributions, particularly if the buyer uses performance specifications. In this study session we will introduce the fairly recent concepts of early buyer involvement (EBI) and early supplier involvement (ESI).

Many people, particularly those who traditionally write specifications, such as users and engineers, think that specifications are entirely their domain. Challenge them: you too can make a major contribution!

Session learning objectives

After completing this session you should be able to:

9.1 Explain the nature of the contribution that buyers and suppliers can make to the specification process.
9.2 Explain the concept of early buyer involvement including liaison with users and the need to understand the user's requirements.
9.3 Explain the concept of early supplier involvement.

Unit content coverage

This study session covers the following topics from the official CIPS unit content document:

Learning outcome

Contribute towards preparing supplier specifications.

Explain policy and information requirements of the organisation when preparing specifications.

Learning objective

2.4 Describe how buyers and suppliers can contribute towards effective specification development.
 • Liaison with users
 • Understanding the user's needs
 • Understanding the legal implications
 • Minimising the tolerances

Prior knowledge

Study sessions 7 and 8.

Resources

None specific but a working knowledge of specification procedures in your workplace would be useful.

Timing

You should set aside about 2 hours to read and complete this session, including learning activities, self-assessment questions, the suggested further reading (if any) and the revision question.

9.1 The contribution that buyers and suppliers can make to the specification process

Here we focus on non-technical contributions to specifications.

It is often the user of the product or service who prepares the specification rather than the purchasing and supply function. This is understandable because users will often say, quite rightly, that they know what item or material they need to perform a particular function or fulfil a particular purpose. In service-based organisations it is likely to be the departments that actually provide the service that will try to insist that they develop specifications *their* way.

This is not to suggest in any way that users/engineers/operations departments and so on are not capable of developing sound *technical* specifications, but a good *overall* specification is a combination of engineering (or function) considerations and commercial ones. This means that buyers need to be aware of the common problems found in specifications that are written by people who may not be commercially aware. Such problems add unnecessary cost or risk to the organisation (see study session 2).

Learning activity 9.1

Try to find an example of a specification in your workplace that has been drafted without any commercial input. Note down any purchasing and supply problems you can find that are caused by this 'technical only' specification, and check your answer with the text that follows.

Feedback on page 95

Here are some common problems with specifications that buyers need to be aware of and be prepared, where necessary, to examine and solve.

- Writing specifications around a particular item, thus preventing competition. This often arises from 'custom and practice' and the fact that users have not been made aware of possible alternatives available from supply markets that may provide cost advantage.
- Looking for a custom built item when acceptable standard items are available.
- Specifying something that does not exist in the marketplace, or which will be difficult to source.
- Over-specifying, for example using unnecessarily tight tolerances, or extra functions that are not necessary. Tolerances were described in study session 7.
- Sometimes many very similar specifications exist but with each one being slightly different from the others. It can lead to a wide range of similar goods being used, and this is a situation where variety reduction, leading to the use of, for example, one part instead of six, would yield great advantage in terms of:
  - consolidation of purchases
  - supply base reduction
  - less stockholding.
- Occasionally, suppliers' representatives will go directly to users and convince them that their product is the one that should be used, leading to specifications being written around the supplier's product specification. This ignores the possibility that other suppliers might offer something just as good but at a lower price.
- The issues discussed in this section will be developed in the next two sections.

9

Self-assessment question 9.1

There follows a short questionnaire. Apply it to one of the specifications from your workplace and answer each question 'yes', 'no' or 'don't know'.

1 In your opinion, is it over-specified?
2 Does it 'tie' you to one supplier?
3 Does it specify a branded item?
4 Does it specify something that would need to be specially manufactured?
5 Is it readily available in the marketplace?
6 Would it have to be imported when, in your opinion, there are suitable UK-made substitutes?
7 Are there similar alternatives that might do the job just as well and are cheaper/more readily available?

Feedback on page 95

9.2 Early buyer involvement (EBI)

As you will have seen, the purchasing department has little input in the specification process in some organisations, the buyer merely receiving specifications from users and sourcing the products or services specified. We are not suggesting that purchasing *take over* the specification process, but there are some strong arguments as to why it should be involved:

- All purchases have a commercial aspect as well as a technical one: even in highly technical purchases such as oil drilling equipment, commercial issues such as maintenance cover, spares availability, warranty period and user training may form part of the specification. These are all areas where purchasing can provide input.
- Purchasing can help identify potential and real supply problems: in practice this will require much discussion with user departments and may not be successful if the user takes the view, in some cases correctly, that the choice of item or material to be used is entirely a technical matter.
- The greatest scope for cost reduction is at the design/specification stage: this concerns trying to ensure that items are not over-specified, as you will have already seen.
- Quality, from the customer's viewpoint, is about more than just technical aspects: for example, when purchasing computer hardware the supplier's response time to maintenance requests is important to internal customer satisfaction. There is little point in having a technically superior product if failures or breakdowns take a long time to fix.
- Communicating product and specification options based on knowledge of the supply market.
- Advising on the appropriate type of specification to use (see study session 8).

For these reasons, purchasing and supply should be involved early on in the process of defining specifications, and should not simply wait to act once a user issues a completed specification. This process, coming to the fore increasingly, is known as **early buyer involvement (EBI)**.

The ability of buyers to make a contribution here depends on their knowledge of specifications, but purchasing staff should know about specifications because:

- Their primary purpose is to contribute to an organisation's profitability by obtaining the best quality products or services in terms of fitness for purpose and the least possible total cost.
- Purchasing staff are intermediaries between the user and the supplier and are, therefore, responsible for checking the completeness of product or service specifications. When negotiating with suppliers, purchasing staff must know what they are negotiating for.
- The satisfaction of user needs depends on obtaining reliable suppliers.
- Purchasing staff should be expert at the provision, at the design or specification stage, of innovative suggestions aimed at achieving cost reduction without detriment to the required performance, reliability, quality and maintainability (of the product).
- Purchasing staff should be able to advise on whether or not any of the requirements stated in the specification are liable to cause commercial, environmental or legal problems.

9

Additionally, there are factors that need to be taken into account when purchasing internationally. For example:

- Language, and the different meaning of certain terms in different languages.
- National standards, regulations and codes of practice, some of which may be required by law.

Learning activity 9.2

Reflect on your reading of this section and compare the procedures from your workplace with the stated principles.

Feedback on page 95

We will now try to develop this a little further.

Self-assessment question 9.2

Try to identify and note down what scope, if any, exists for the development of EBI in your organisation and how you would contribute to it. If there is no scope, write a report on how you would develop and contribute to EBI.

Feedback on page 95

9.3 Early supplier involvement (ESI)

The supplier's role in preparing specifications

It may also be appropriate to get suppliers involved early in the process of determining specifications. This process is known as **early supplier involvement (ESI)**. It is something that is often seen as a development of EBI (see section 9.2 above) because buyers can suggest that suppliers be brought into the design/specification process to add their expertise.

ESI would be most useful when the supplier possesses important technical expertise or experience that the buying organisation does not have. The likelihood of arriving at an innovative solution for the specification that reduces cost or lead time, for example, will be significantly improved with the benefit of the supplier's input. In referring to 'the supplier' here, we mean tried and tested suppliers with whom we have worked closely for some time.

At a simplistic level, ESI might involve something such as a supplier stating that they can supply a 'standard' part instead of the 'special' part requested by the buyer. On the other hand, ESI might involve holding discussions with a supplier with whom you have a close, long-standing relationship at the design/specification stage to incorporate the supplier's expertise into the design.

ESI is routinely used in the service sector, where service providers are often called in by buying organisations to assess what is needed so that a specification for the service, for example, IT support, is drafted as a joint effort.

Problems with ESI

In the main, these concern over-reliance on one supplier and the possibility that, over time, your organisation might become so dependent on the supplier that it is impossible to change suppliers if the supplier stops giving you the quality and service that you require and once were receiving.

Learning activity 9.3

Reflect on your reading of the text and think about whether ESI is used at your workplace. If it is used, note down what items or services it is used for, how it works and whether it gives similar advantages to those described in the text.

Feedback on page 96

You can now develop some of your thoughts on this topic via the following self-assessment question.

Self-assessment question 9.3

Your organisation intends to install an enterprise resource planning (ERP) system (this links all of the organisation's departments electronically, allowing access to information and a common database). These are very expensive, complex systems, and you want to obtain the best advice before installing it. To this end, you have suggested that your long-standing IT support provider should be brought in at the initial stage to give advice.

Write a report to your line manager on the kind of advice you expect your IT support provider to give.

Feedback on page 96

Revision question

Now try the revision question for this session on page 196.

Summary

In this study session we have continued to look at specifications, with the objective of considering the role of buyers and suppliers in developing specifications. We have made strong arguments for the inclusion of both parties in the process of specification development, focusing on:

- The fact that specifications usually have commercial as well as technical aspects.
- Typical advantages arising from commercial contribution are:
  - cost savings
  - better technical specification (from ESI)
  - early identification of potential problems
  - reduction of over-specifying
  - the buyer being better able to use supply market competition.

Suggested further reading

You might like to read about these issues in more detail in chapters 8 and 9 of Lysons and Farrington (2006).

Feedback on learning activities and self-assessment questions

Feedback on learning activity 9.1

If you are able to find such a specification the kind of problems you might be able to identify are:

- Over-specification, although you might find this difficult to identify unless you have considerable experience.
- Specification that effectively 'ties' you to one supplier.
- Specifying something that is very difficult to find in the market.
- Specification of a 'special' when there are standard items available that will probably perform the required function adequately.

Feedback on self-assessment question 9.1

The answers you give will depend entirely on your choice of specification and your working environment. If four or more of your answers were 'yes' you should try to suggest to the user departments/technical staff that the specification be examined to see whether it can be changed to take account of some of the commercial issues mentioned in the text, such as wide availability, changing it to a standard item and so on.

Feedback on learning activity 9.2

Specific feedback is difficult because of the individual nature of your workplace, but you may have identified that EBI is performed much as is suggested in the text. On the other hand, EBI might not be used at all. It could be that, instead of using EBI per se, your organisation encourages you to challenge specifications where you feel it necessary.

Feedback on self-assessment question 9.2

Again, much depends here on the actual scope in your organisation for the use of EBI. If it already exists to a high degree, you should have identified that you can contribute information on issues with commercial implications, such as maintenance possibilities, guarantee terms, after-sales service and so on.

If EBI does not exist in your organisation but you think there is much scope for it, you could identify that you would need to get all interested parties together and discuss the concept of EBI and its benefits so that it might be developed on a multifunctional basis.

One important aspect that is worth mentioning is that the setting up and development of EBI might require the effective 'selling' of the purchasing function so that technical staff realise that benefits can be gained by using EBI and the expertise of buyers.

Feedback on learning activity 9.3

Specific feedback is difficult, but if ESI is used, advantages should include:

- Use of supplier's expertise to give better technical features at the best price.
- Early identification of potential cost savings.
- Suggestions from the supplier of different/better ways of achieving product/service goals.
- For service provision it is highly likely that service providers would be brought in to advise on the requirements that the service would address.

Feedback on self-assessment question 9.3

You do not need to comment specifically on the workings of ERP but the kind of advice that you would expect to receive would be:

- What systems are available on the market (there are several: SAP, PeopleSoft, and so on).
- Relative prices.
- Relative strengths and weaknesses.
- Ease of operation of each system.
- How good/available is maintenance and other support.
- How easily the respective systems could be updated.

9

Information requirements for effective specifications

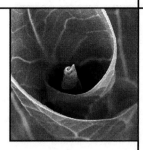

'Suits *you* sir!' But does it and is it the best value?

Introduction

Many buyers, at both a personal level and an organisational level, like to buy 'bespoke' items or services: that is, made to measure or tailored. The idea is that something made to measure will fit better and will look better, but is this always necessary? Is there any point in paying a high price for an item or service if a 'standard' one will do just as well? Services will usually be bespoke, by definition, because they will be performed to your requirements on your premises. But some services, for example payroll or cleaning, will essentially be 'standard', but 'tweaked' a little to suit your requirements.

Session learning objectives

After completing this session you should be able to:

10.1 Identify information relating to possible suppliers.
10.2 Describe the technical requirements for different types of purchase such as projects, materials and services.
10.3 Describe timescales, costs and budgets for expenditure and delivery requirements.

Unit content coverage

This study session covers the following topics from the official CIPS unit content document:

Learning outcome

Contribute towards preparing supplier specifications.

Explain policy and information requirements of the organisation when preparing specifications.

Learning objective

2.5 Explain information requirements for developing effective specifications – possible suppliers:
• Technical requirements: project specifications, material specifications
• Timelines: schedules
• Delivery requirements for supply: times required

Prior knowledge

Study sessions 7, 8 and 9.

10

Timing

You should set aside about 2¼ hours to read and complete this session, including learning activities, self-assessment questions, the suggested further reading (if any) and the revision question.

10.1 'Bespoke' (made to order) versus 'standard' (readily available)

Many specifications that you will encounter will require the supply of specially made items or equipment. In many cases this will be necessary, and there is nothing intrinsically wrong with it. However, there are many situations that do not require specially made items.

The tone here suggests that specially made items are a 'bad thing', but this is not necessarily the case. There are situations where only a specially made thing will do the job as required. However, there are likely to be many situations in your career where a supply market standard – that is, something that already exists in the supply market – will do the job perfectly well.

The 'trick' here is for the buyer to be aware of such situations and make appropriate recommendations to users when it appears that advantages would be gained. Such advantages would usually concern price and availability: in other words, supply market 'standard' items are usually cheaper and more readily available than specially made items. They are also likely to be available from several suppliers, whereas 'specials', by definition, come from only one supplier, although such items could normally be re-sourced, if necessary.

Learning activity 10.1

In your workplace identify whether any 'special' items are being purchased when there might be 'standard' items available. If so, what might be the reasons for this?

Feedback on page 103

How can buyers try to change this state of affairs?

The most important element here is knowledge about the supply market. You should try to gain as much knowledge as you can about your major supply markets so that you know, without needing to check, who supplies what, and what variations there are in their product lines. You should then try to input this knowledge into the specification process whenever it is relevant to do so. This could be part of the EBI process you will have seen in study session 9.

You can gain this kind of knowledge from:

- frequent visits to suppliers
- discussions with suppliers' representatives
- visits to *relevant* trade exhibitions.

10

We have tended to concentrate on products rather than services. Services, generally by their nature, are 'special' but you should try to be aware of standard services such as cleaning or security that might be suitable for your requirements and try to have them used, where possible.

Self-assessment question 10.1

Write a memorandum to your subordinates indicating why 'standards' are generally better than 'specials' but indicating why 'specials' are sometimes necessary. Use your workplace experience if it is relevant.

Feedback on page 103

10.2 The technical requirements for different types of purchase: materials, services, and so on

So far, we have discussed specifications at great length and established that specifications indicate what quality is required. But what characteristics of products and services contribute to 'quality'?

Product quality

D A Gavin has provided a useful vocabulary for describing product quality characteristics:

- **Performance**: primary operating characteristics.
- **Features**: the 'bells and whistles' – extras provided that are not essential to the product's performance.
- **Conformance**: the degree to which the design matches known or agreed standards.
- **Reliability**: the likelihood of failure in a given time period.
- **Durability**: the useful life of the product.
- **Serviceability**: speed, ease and cost of maintenance.
- **Aesthetics**: the look, feel, sound, taste and smell of a product.
- **Perceived quality**: brand image and reputation.

The prioritisation or importance of each of these characteristics will vary from product to product. Buyers may need to discuss with users the question of which characteristics to prioritise. Certainly, to be able to develop a meaningful specification, information on all of these characteristics would be required.

Learning activity 10.2

Consider a personal computer, a forklift truck and a light bulb. Note down what you would regard as the three most important quality characteristics of each one, in no particular order.

Feedback on page 103

10

Service quality

As you will have already noted, in study session 8 for example, specifications for services are much more difficult to write than they are for products. However, Parasuraman, a writer on service quality, has provided us with a set of quality characteristics for services:

- **Reliability**: consistency of performance and dependability, meaning that the firm performs the service right first time and honours its promises.
- **Responsiveness**: the willingness and readiness of employees to provide the service, including timeliness.
- **Competence**: the required skills and knowledge to perform the service.
- **Access**: approachability and ease of contact.
- **Courtesy**: politeness, respect, consideration and friendliness of contact personnel including receptionists and telephonists.
- **Communication**: keeping customers informed in a language they can understand, which may mean adjusting it for different customers.
- **Credibility**: trustworthiness, honesty and believability – having the customer's best interests at heart.
- **Security**: freedom from danger, risk or doubt.
- **Understanding**: making the effort to understand the customer's needs
- **Tangibles**: physical evidence of the service.

10

Self-assessment question 10.2

Based on the above service quality characteristics, write a short specification to be used to advertise a security service contract for your premises.

Feedback on page 104

10.3 Timescales, costs and budgets for expenditure

This introduces the concept of **contract management**, a process that ensures a contract is performed to a standard that fully meets the objectives and expectations agreed between the purchaser and the supplier. Effective contract management does not simply start from the award of a contract; the process runs from the identification of the requirement through to the completion of the contract.

In terms of our objectives in contract management, there are three essential requirements for any contract, whether it is for the procurement of a product or a service. These are to obtain the right quality, the right timing and all at the right total cost. Sometimes greater emphasis is placed on one of these objectives at the expense of another. For example, the organisation may be experiencing financial difficulties, which would exert pressure on financial budgets, and so a key requirement may be to reduce costs at the expense of quality and timing. Alternatively, the work may be required as an emergency and so, in an effort to get the work done, cost may not be the key priority.

Budgets

These are normally drafted as a result of collaboration between the user, purchaser and contract/project manager. Their purpose is to try to identify costs in advance and ensure that funds will be available to meet them. Purchasing should provide information on projected material costs as well as on costs relating to any subcontract element of the contract or project. Budgets should not normally be 'cast in stone' because contracts, particularly those relating to major projects, often encounter cost overruns, and without a mechanism for dealing with these the contract/project might founder.

Contract management places a high priority on achieving *value for money*. This is a balance of cost, risk, delivery and quality. The specification requesting suppliers to quote for any contract should state the purchaser's requirements clearly. Effective contract management then helps to secure *value for money* by:

- Recording and controlling the cost of the product or service bought.
- Ensuring timely delivery. For projects this would involve constructing a timeline (a projection of the order in which each task should be completed, including 'milestones', which are important stages that must be reached before he next stage is started).
- Ensuring that the risks (what could go wrong) are fully identified.
- Ensuring quality of the product or service bought.

Effective contract management prevents such problems from occurring. It requires both before effort the contract is placed and controls set in place once the contract is under way.

The relationship with the supplier has a great deal of impact on the actual results achieved once the contract is in progress. Teamwork is necessary with the supplier to achieve the results that are required. There needs to be collaboration with the supplier, and the problems that can often arise in contracts need to be solved. Communication between the organisations involved is important.

Learning activity 10.3

Think about some major contracts or projects at work and note down whether any organised project or contract management takes place. If it does exist, what form does it take?

Feedback on page 104

Having attempted the learning activity now attempt the following:

Self-assessment question 10.3

As purchasing manager you are about to meet users and the finance manager to develop a budget for the supply of a suite of personal computers to your organisation.

Write notes on the aspects you would cover and the information you would need to contribute to this process.

Feedback on page 104

Revision question

Now try the revision question for this session on page 196.

Summary

In this study session we have considered some more aspects of specifications. Specifically, this has included considering why items available as 'standards' will often represent better purchases than items made specially for you. The main reasons are:

- 'Standards' will usually be cheaper than specials.
- They will usually be more readily available.
- They will usually be available from a number of suppliers.

Also, we have considered the differences between product quality characteristics and service quality characteristics, product quality characteristics being:

- performance
- features
- conformance
- reliability
- durability
- serviceability
- aesthetics
- perceived quality.

Characteristics of service quality are:

- reliability
- responsiveness
- competence
- access
- courtesy
- communication.
- credibility
- security

- understanding
- tangibles.

We have also introduced contract management, which is important to ensure that any major, long-term contract runs smoothly and in accordance with the wishes of both parties.

Suggested further reading

Chapters 8 and 9 of Lysons and Farrington (2006) should give you some more insight into the issues discussed in this study session.

Feedback on learning activities and self-assessment questions

Feedback on learning activity 10.1

It is impossible to give specific feedback on the first part, but typical reasons for such a state of affairs might be:

- A 'special' is genuinely required because of the singular nature of the requirement.
- Lack of knowledge about the supply market.
- Lack of a forum whereby any supply market knowledge that exists can be fed into the decision-making process.
- Users having developed their own specifications, in isolation, for years and refusing to allow buyers to contribute to the process.

Feedback on self-assessment question 10.1

Your report should focus on the fact that standard items from the supply market are usually:

- more readily available than 'specials'
- cheaper
- available from a wide range of suppliers
- more easily replaceable.

However, 'specials' may sometimes be necessary because there is no standard item available to fulfil the function required. In such situations it may be worth challenging the actual requirement.

Feedback on learning activity 10.2

Answers to this activity would be subjective to some extent but should be along the following lines:

- Personal computer: performance, features and aesthetics. Serviceability and perceived quality might appear also.
- Forklift truck: performance, serviceability and durability. Features and reliability might also appear.

10

- Light bulb: conformance, reliability and durability. It is difficult to imagine any others here; performance is a 'given' and aesthetics are unlikely to feature.

Feedback on self-assessment question 10.2

You could have included the following in your specification:

- Reliability: all staff to be present ten minutes before the start of the shift and not finish until the relief shift has arrived.
- Responsiveness: respond to all alarm calls within ten minutes.
- Competence: demonstrate that all officers have up-to-date training.
- Access: provide a 24-hour emergency number for contact.
- Courtesy: security staff must treat your company's employees with respect.
- Communication: report daily to your operations manager and write a weekly incident report.
- Credibility: all incidents occurring should remain confidential.
- Security: any change to normal service must be communicated to the operations manager with ten days' notice.
- Understanding: security staff should deal differently with staff queries and visitor queries.
- Tangibles: all security staff should wear uniform.

Your exact details under each heading may be different from this guide but should be along similar lines.

Feedback on learning activity 10.3

Specific feedback is impossible because of the nature of the activity. Your organisation should, ideally, ensure that a manager is delegated to act as project manager for any major contract, particularly long-term projects.

Alternatively, you might have one person, perhaps with a small department, appointed as 'contract manager', whose role would be to manage the progress of all contracts/projects.

The worst possibility is if there is no contract/project management at all and contracts are merely 'left to their own devices'.

Feedback on self-assessment question 10.3

It is possible that the budget process might be combined with evaluation of potential suppliers, so you might go to the meeting armed with comparative information using data from different potential suppliers.

However, the kind of information you need would be:

- Cost of the hardware (or costs, if comparisons are to be made).
- Costs of any peripherals such as printers.
- Cost(s) of any software packages that might be essential or desirable.
- Support and maintenance costs as indicated by the supplier(s).

10

- Costs of consumables such as printer paper, CDs and floppy disks.
- Costs of energy, if this last one can be calculated.

You might be able to think of other costs that should be included.

10

10

Internal and external influences on specifications

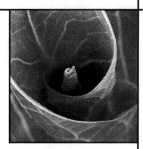

Introduction

In this study session we shall consider the effects of organisational policies relating to corporate social responsibility, ethical behaviour and conflict of interests on specifications. We shall also examine published standards such as kitemarks and the need for specifications to match up to them, as well as considering pricing and payment practices. All of these issues might find their way into specifications: for example, a specification might stipulate that raw materials such as timber that make up a purchased product be purchased by the product supplier from sustainable, managed resources.

'We're given a code to live our lives by. We don't always follow it, but it's still there.'
Gary Oldman

Session learning objectives

After completing this session you should be able to:

11.1 Explain the important concepts of corporate social responsibility (CSR)/ethics/conflict of interest.
11.2 Describe quality kitemarks/processes/procedures.
11.3 Give examples of pricing and payment practices.

Unit content coverage

This study session covers the following topics from the official CIPS unit content document:

Learning outcome

Contribute towards preparing supplier specifications.

Explain policy and information requirements of the organisation when preparing specifications.

Learning objective

2.6 Identify areas within specifications where legislation and company policy might impact upon the development of purchasing specifications.
- Corporate social responsibility, ethics, conflict of interest
- Quality kitemarks, processes, procedures
- Minimum standards of practice and performance

Prior knowledge

Study sessions 7, 8, 9 and 10.

11

Resources

None specific although good knowledge of organisational practices would be useful

Timing

You should set aside about 2¼ hours to read and complete this session, including learning activities, self-assessment questions, the suggested further reading (if any) and the revision question.

11.1 Corporate social responsibility, ethics and conflict of interest

A professional buyer should operate to a certain code of ethics, both within and outside the company. This is primarily so that suppliers will recognise the integrity and fairness of the purchasing operation and make their offers accordingly.

Typically an ethical code will include:

- The buyer should be fair when dealing with suppliers.
- The buyer should respect the confidentiality of information provided by the supplier. For example, tender information should be treated as confidential and kept securely. Where it is considered reasonable to reveal certain information, it should not be traceable back to the particular supplier unless the supplier has given permission.
- The buyer should not mislead suppliers.
- The buyer should not engage in 'Dutch auctions' (that is, where a buyer discloses Supplier X's price to Supplier Y to get Supplier Y to beat the price, then discloses Supplier Y's new price to Supplier X to get Supplier X's price down, and so on).
- The buyer should not unfairly pressurise a supplier.
- There should be transparency of why particular suppliers were invited to quote or tender.
- There should be transparency of criteria for selecting suppliers.
- There should be transparency of how the bids were evaluated against the criteria, and the successful supplier chosen.
- All suppliers should be treated equally. For example, any additional information given to one supplier in response to a question on an invitation to tender should be provided to all other suppliers.
- Buyers should not give or receive any bribes, gifts or special hospitality.
- Buyers should declare any interest in a particular supplier.

Learning activity 11.1

Try to find out whether your organisation has a written ethical code. It might be in your purchasing manual or you might have to discuss it with

(continued on next page)

Learning activity 11.1 *(continued)*

colleagues. Note down to what extent it coincides with the guidelines you have just seen.

Feedback on page 112

Ethical sourcing

Many companies are under increasing pressure from customers to operate ethical sourcing policies, which come under the general heading of **corporate social responsibility (CSR)**. This refers to issues such as:

- child labour
- forced labour
- low wages
- poor working conditions
- inadequate health and safety
- intimidation of workers defending their rights.

Mistakes in this area can result in very bad publicity for a company. An example of this was GAP Clothing Stores, which received some bad publicity a few years ago because they *allegedly* used suppliers that did not conform to these guidelines. The problem here is that such allegations might be unfounded, but the fact that they are known to have been made causes bad and potentially damaging publicity.

Self-assessment question 11.1

Draft a report to senior management on why there should be a policy relating to CSR, including making a business case.

Feedback on page 112

11.2 Quality standards and 'kite marks'

This section will include the need for specifications to measure up to published standards.

We covered standards in study session 8 but you should be aware that some standards have the force of law. This means that any specifications used for items that fall into such categories must comply with any relevant standard, examples of which include:

- Control of Substances Hazardous to Health (COSHH)
- 'Kitemarks': these denote that the item has been produced in line with a particular standard and usually relate to issues of safety.

Additionally, legislation might cover the production and use of items and materials that might impact upon the environment, such as:

- waste disposal
- chemicals

11

- herbicides
- solvents
- flammable/explosive materials.

If a product or service needs to comply with any legislation, it is up to the team developing the specification to ensure that the specification includes the legal requirements. The role of the buyer in this respect is twofold:

- ensuring that information that originates in the supply market is communicated to the specification team
- ensuring that any legal requirements are clearly communicated to the supplier.

Additionally, if the company has policies that might affect specifications, the buyer needs to ensure that these are communicated to suppliers and incorporated into the products supplied.

Learning activity 11.2

Select five specifications that are in use at work and ascertain whether they measure up to published standards. What standards are involved? If the specifications do not measure up, what are the reasons for this?

Feedback on page 112

Now try this:

Self-assessment question 11.2

A challenging one! Try to develop a questionnaire that you could ask potential suppliers to complete to confirm their ability to produce items or provide services that do not adversely affect the environment. You may use any similar document already existing in your organisation to assist you.

Feedback on page 113

11.3 Pricing and payment practices and their effect on specifications

Introduction

You will have studied the idea of 'paying the right price' in study session 6. Here, we need to consider the potential effect on specifications of how we decide what is the right price and how we pay for goods and services.

Pricing

In study session 6 we highlighted the fact that price and quality are inextricably linked and are usually thought of as relating to *value*. The message we should take from this is that, if we want good quality or quality that conforms to particular standards such as the kitemarks we considered in the last section, we must be prepared to pay for it. This may include paying a premium price for such quality. If we are not prepared to pay in this way, we may need to rethink our views on what is the 'right' quality.

Payment

You may not associate payment with quality and specifications. However, you should be aware that suppliers depend on prompt payment for their cashflow and that, if this does not happen, they might need to 'cut corners', which could have a detrimental effect on their quality.

Learning activity 11.3

Consider how payments are made where you work. Are there situations where your organisation deliberately pays late? If so, why might this be?

Feedback on page 113

Some buyers have the opinion that late payment to suppliers is a 'good thing' because it helps the purchaser's cashflow. However, you are not doing your organisation any favours if, because of late payment, a supplier's quality starts to fall away. You might say that you are not directly responsible for payments, but you should do everything you can to ensure that the people responsible for payment know that they need to make payments promptly.

11

Self-assessment question 11.3

One day you receive a letter from Exodus Ltd, your catering provider, informing you that their last invoice, which was sent to you three months ago, has not been paid. They ask you to investigate why this might be the case. Upon asking the credit control manager, who has direct responsibility for making payments to suppliers, you find that your company has a cashflow problem and that no invoices have been paid for several weeks. The credit control manager says that your company is unable to settle invoices for at least the next four weeks.

What would you expect to be the consequences of this situation both as far as Exodus Ltd is concerned and as far as other suppliers are concerned, in terms of their dealings with you?

Feedback on page 113

Revision question

Now try the revision question for this session on page 197.

Summary

In this study session we have tried to link specifications with the increasingly important considerations of ethics and CSR. One of the most important things that you should have learned in this session is that everything is related and that virtually nothing in purchasing and supply exists in isolation. Specifically, we have considered:

- The main aspects of ethics and CSR, identifying what they both mean to buyers.
- The effect of standards and means of identifying them such as kitemarks
- The effect of the price we pay and the way we pay it on quality and specifications.

Suggested further reading

You may have already read about quality and specifications from reading suggestions in previous study sessions. You might want to read more about ethics and CSR in chapter 17 of Lysons and Farrington (2006).

Feedback on learning activities and self-assessment questions

Feedback on learning activity 11.1

Feedback cannot be specific because all organisations will be different. If you do not have a code of ethics as such, you might have company policy on such things as tendering procedures that forbid the use of 'Dutch auctions' and not receiving excessive hospitality or large gifts. You might also have policies on such things as clear selection criteria for selecting suppliers. This will be covered (for large purchases) by EU directives if you work in a public sector organisation.

Feedback on self-assessment question 11.1

You might find this a difficult self-assessment question, but if you have thought about the subject you might have identified some of the following points:

- There are more and more pressure groups trying to influence people's thinking about CSR.
- If your competitors have a CSR programme and you do not, you are likely to lose out to your competitors.
- Many large companies such as Adidas and Nike have received much bad publicity because of *alleged* unethical sourcing.

Feedback on learning activity 11.2

It is impossible to make an exhaustive list of such specifications. However, for example, 13 amp plugs should be made to comply with BS 1363, so if you work for a manufacturer of electrical products, including plugs, your specifications must comply with this standard.

11

Possible reasons for specifications not complying in this way could be that your organisation believes that the published standard is not rigorous enough to suit your specific need. An example would be the way that the motor industry uses QS 9000 as an alternative to ISO 9000 because it does not believe that the latter is rigorous enough, although we should point out that these standards do not have the force of law. Another possible reason for non-compliance might be that the items are produced solely for export to countries where, for example, kitemarks do not apply.

Feedback on self-assessment question 11.2

This is a difficult one. There is no 'correct' answer; phrasing is always an individual matter, and your organisation's needs would probably be unique, but here is an example:

1   What is your environmental policy?
2   Do you operate an environmental management system such as ISO 14000?
3   What environmental considerations do you make in selecting your suppliers?
4   If you do not currently have an environmental policy or environmental management system, what plans do you have to introduce them?

Feedback on learning activity 11.3

Some organisations habitually pay suppliers late. The reasons given for this are usually that it is seen to improve the purchaser's cashflow or that it acts as a kind of extra discount because the purchaser can keep their money in the bank for longer and earn interest. Of course, it could just be down to lack of money, particularly for large payments, or organisational inertia.

Hopefully, your organisation would not be one of these and pays its bills on time.

Feedback on self-assessment question 11.3

This one needs some creativity. Possible consequences depend on your relationships with Exodus Ltd and other suppliers. If the relationships are good you might be able to persuade them to await payment by reassuring them that payment will be made. If relationships are not so good, Exodus Ltd might 'down tools' and walk off your site, meaning that your company would be without catering, a situation your workforce would be extremely unhappy with.

As far as your other suppliers are concerned, they might put you 'on the stop list' (in other words, would refuse to supply you) until their invoices had been settled. This would sour any relationships you had developed with suppliers, and mean that you would need to find alternative sources of supply to keep the company operating. Any such alternative suppliers would need to be ones that did not know that you were experiencing cashflow problems.

11

11

Study session 12

The purchasing 'cycle'

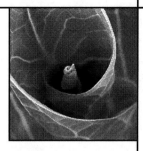

Introduction

The purchasing 'cycle' is all of the procurement activities that take place from the initial identification of need to the final satisfaction of that need. This includes writing specifications, soliciting quotations from suppliers, order placing, receiving the goods, paying for them and 'rating' the supplier, among other activities.

'Like a circle in a spiral, like a wheel within a wheel, never ending or beginning…'.
Alan Bergman/Michel Legrand

Session learning objectives

After completing this session you should be able to:

12.1 Describe the processes of identification of needs and the establishment of the specification.
12.2 Summarise methods of surveying the market, selecting the most promising suppliers and appraising suppliers.
12.3 Demonstrate how to invite quotations, analyse them and select the most promising supplier.
12.4 Explain how to negotiate the best value for money and award the contract.
12.5 Explain how to monitor, review and maintain performance.

Unit content coverage

This study session covers the following topics from the official CIPS unit content document:

Learning outcome

Outline the stages of identifying and sourcing suppliers

Learning objective

3.1 Identify the different stages of sourcing suppliers:
• Identify the needs
• Establish the specification
• Survey the market
• Source the market
• Appraise (audit) suppliers
• Invite quotations (tenders)
• Analyse quotations and select the most promising supplier
• Negotiate the best value for money
• Award the contract
• Monitor, review and maintain performance

12

Prior knowledge

None although previous sessions might be of use, particularly study session 7 – study session 11.

Resources

None specific although internet access would be useful for some learning activities.

Timing

You should set aside about 2¾ hours to read and complete this session, including learning activities, self-assessment questions, the suggested further reading (if any) and the revision question.

12.1 Identification of needs and specification development

Before we consider these stages in the purchasing cycle it would be useful to have a diagrammatic illustration of the 'cycle'. This is shown in figure 12.1.

Figure 12.1: The purchasing cycle

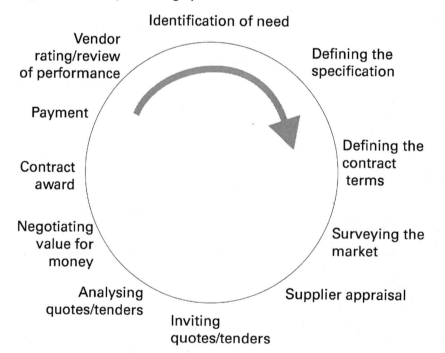

Identification of need

This is the first stage in the purchasing process and occurs when someone in the buyer's organisation, usually a user/budget holder, realises that they need something. This might be something entirely new or it might be something that has been purchased many times before. A good example of the latter would be the replenishment of stock items in the stores.

Buyers may have a role to play in this process by suggesting items that are standard (as opposed to 'special'), readily available in the market and represent good value, although you should realise that, in some situations, the user will need something that does not quite fit these considerations.

Once the need has been identified it will be transmitted to the purchasing department by means of a purchase requisition. Traditionally these were written, but today they are much more likely to be electronic.

Learning activity 12.1

Write down what you believe are the main pieces of information that a purchase requisition should contain. Use your own experience if necessary or discuss it with colleagues.

Feedback on page 122

Establishment of the specification

Once the need has been identified the next step is to develop a suitable specification for it. Specifications were covered in some depth in study sessions 7 – 11 but it is important that whatever type of specification is used, it adequately describes the need and is one that the supply market will recognise.

Self-assessment question 12.1

Write a report of not more than 200 words to colleagues on how buyers might be able to contribute to the need identification process, and note down any specific contributions that you have been able to make in the past.

Feedback on page 122

12

12.2 Surveying the market, selecting the most promising supplier and supplier appraisal

These stages generally take place only if the item/service to be purchased has never been purchased by your organisation before. You may note that the purchasing cycle diagram in section 12.1 gives 'defining the contract terms' as the stage after developing the specification. These are usually a 'standard' set of terms defined by the organisation's management and are used with all purchases. We shall consider contractual terms in study session 18.

Surveying the market

This process is often known as 'sourcing', and is the process of identifying suppliers that are able to supply the goods or services purchasers require.

There are several sources of information to find potential sources of supply:

- Supplier information file: the buyer may keep records of details of possible suppliers.
- Supplier catalogues: these provide a quick and efficient guide to the availability of suppliers for more standardised requirements. Remember, though, that they are also advertising material.
- Trade registers and directories: Kompass, Rylands as well as Dun & Bradstreet (and other) directories provide alphabetical and commodity-based information.
- Trade exhibitions: these may provide opportunities to see innovations and new suppliers.
- Other purchasing organisations: *may* be willing to offer advice, although this is unlikely if they are competitors of your organisation.
- Internet: widely and increasingly used because it provides an easily accessible worldwide database.

Learning activity 12.2

Think about an item or service that you have sourced in the past using 'traditional' means such as your record files, trade directories and so on. Try sourcing it on the internet and note down the differences you find. You might find it helpful to use the website http://www.comparestoreprices.co.uk as a starting point.

Feedback on page 122

Selecting the most promising suppliers

Here the buyer selects what appear to be the most promising suppliers from those identified from the various sources of information on potential suppliers that we have just seen.

Appraising suppliers

Before inviting quotations from potential suppliers, we need to be as sure as we can be that these companies will be capable of providing us with the right quality of product/service, at the right time and in a way that represents good value. This is so that only suppliers that are judged competent will be requested to provide quotations. We can find out about potential sources by appraising them, usually by means of obtaining references, use of questionnaires and visits to their premises. We shall examine the detail of these processes in study session 13.

Self-assessment question 12.2

For some time you have been having problems with a supplier who carries out plastic coating of small fabrications that you send to them in small quantities on a regular basis. Essentially, the main problem is the frequent

(continued on next page)

Self-assessment question 12.2 *(continued)*

poor quality of the work, for which the supplier blames the nature of the surface of the fabrications.

Your production manager informs you that he has located a company that can provide an alternative powder coating process without the quality problems previously experienced.

You send a consignment of fabrications to this supplier, but three days later the production manager wants to know why they have not returned. You check with the supplier and are informed that you have sent 20 fabrications whereas the minimum batch quantity is 100 and that the supplier will not be able to complete the job until 100 fabrications have been sent.

Explain why this situation has arisen.

Feedback on page 123

12.3 Inviting and analysing quotations

When we have selected several competent suppliers for the product or service we wish to purchase it is usual to send each of them a **request for quotation (RFQ)**, sometimes known as an enquiry.

The RFQ will contain information such as the quantity, description, date required, and so on. When the suppliers submit their quotations based on the RFQ information the buyer compares them and decides which supplier appears to be the best and, therefore, the one we should purchase from. This decision is often, though not always, made on price grounds. Once the supplier is selected the buyer will send them a purchase order (award a contract). We shall consider this process, which is often known as **tendering**, in much more detail in study session 14.

Learning activity 12.3

Think about your RFQ process at work and note down how many potential suppliers you would typically send an RFQ to. What is the reasoning behind this number? If you do not use the RFQ system, what are the reasons for this?

Feedback on page 123

Now attempt this:

Self-assessment question 12.3

Write a brief report recommending how the RFQ process should be done.

Feedback on page 123

12.4 Negotiation

The purchaser always needs to ensure that value for money is achieved. In more complex purchasing decisions lengthy negotiations can be necessary to guarantee that the supplier fully understands the purchaser's requirements. In addition, there may be aspects of the supplier's quotation or tender that can be improved upon. Costs may be reduced and quality improved by careful negotiations.

Negotiation may take place with what appears to be the 'best' supplier, after the quotation process, to finalise details before awarding the contract to the supplier.

The full detail of negotiation is beyond our scope here, but later in your CIPS studies you will encounter a study unit devoted to it.

Learning activity 12.4

Reflect on your experience of awarding contracts and write down how they are awarded in your organisation. Does your organisation have different procedures for awarding contracts of different values, for example for those with a value under £10, under £100 or over £1,000? Does negotiation take place for every contract?

Feedback on page 123

12

Now attempt this:

Self-assessment question 12.4

Review the following checklist of personal skills/attributes and using your experience and/or asking colleagues as necessary, state which you regard as being the most important in negotiation:

- verbal communication skills
- non-verbal communication skills, including being able to 'read' body language and being able to suppress non-verbal clues
- ability to remain calm and rational
- ability to cope with conflict and emotion
- ability to display self-confidence and assertiveness
- ability to withstand pressure tactics
- ability to be patient and flexible
- ability to reassess a position quickly as the negotiation progresses
- ability to create variations and counter proposals.

Feedback on page 124

12.5 Monitoring and reviewing performance

This section includes post-contract award activities.

Once the contract has been awarded to the supplier the next stages are that the contract will be expedited if necessary, the goods will be received or the service completed and, assuming everything is satisfactory, the supplier's invoice will be paid. The invoice will only be paid when the supplier's invoice is reconciled with the goods received note made out by the goods receiving section or department. Many organisations use IT systems to reconcile these, and some have systems of automatic billing where the whole process is done by computer.

It is then usual and useful to monitor suppliers' performance on an ongoing basis. This can help you judge whether individual purchases have been a success and ensure that you have an up-to-date 'picture' of how good your suppliers are and/or whether they need to improve their service to you. It can also help ensure that, in future, you involve only good, proven suppliers in the RFQ process, and can help develop good relationships with suppliers.

Generally, this process, often known as vendor rating, involves measuring suppliers' performance using price, delivery and quality as the main measurement criteria, although these criteria should be established with suppliers. It can be a detailed process, and we shall examine it in much more detail in study session 15.

Learning activity 12.5

Think about your vendor rating process at work and note down what criteria you use to monitor suppliers. If you do not have a formal vendor rating system, write down why you think this is.

Feedback on page 124

Now attempt this:

Self-assessment question 12.5

For some reason, your chief expediter keeps telling you that some suppliers are being regularly 'delinquent' in terms of delivery service. You are fairly sure in your mind that these suppliers are 'good' suppliers. Write a brief report indicating how you could find out whether these suppliers have delivery problems or whether, as you believe, they provide good service.

Feedback on page 124

Revision question

Now try the revision question for this session on page 197.

12

Summary

In this study session we have considered the concept of the purchasing cycle, with a brief examination of each of its 11 stages. The purchasing cycle is regarded as being very much at the core of purchasing and supply, and *any* purchasing activity could be linked to one of the stages. None of them is more important than the others, but all of them should be balanced against each other and carried out in sequence. You should note the 'circular' nature of the sequence so that, after the performance monitoring stage has taken place, the item will almost certainly be needed again and the whole process will start afresh.

Suggested further reading

You can read about some of the issues in this study session in chapter 11 of Lysons and Farrington (2006) and chapter 18 of Baily et al (2004).

Feedback on learning activities and self-assessment questions

Feedback on learning activity 12.1

A purchase requisition should contain:

- a description of the product or service required
- the quantity required
- the delivery or completion date
- the internal budget/department code to which the expenditure is to be charged
- the date of origination
- the originator's signature.

Also, it should be accompanied by the specification where necessary.

Feedback on self-assessment question 12.1

You should have identified that buyers should be able to contribute market availability issues so that a user may change their requirement from something that would have been difficult to acquire, particularly on a repetitive basis, to something that is readily available. Also, a user might change their requirement from something expensive to something more reasonably priced as a result of buyers' input.

Feedback on learning activity 12.2

Once again, specific feedback is impossible owing to the nature of the activity, but the first thing that you should notice is the large number of companies that can supply the item you are searching for. This is on the assumption that the item/service is of a 'standard' nature. One of the problems with the internet is that it can give you far too much choice, and you have to do much work to reduce the choice to a manageable level. Also,

12

if the item/service is somewhat specialist in nature, the internet can be of limited use unless you can put it into a clear commodity category.

Feedback on self-assessment question 12.2

What has happened here is that the supplier has been selected by the production manager, rather than by the buyer, purely on technical grounds, and no supplier appraisal has been carried out. If such appraisal had been performed it would have identified such issues as minimum batch quantities and turn-round times.

Feedback on learning activity 12.3

There is a traditional view that sending an RFQ to three suppliers is enough, but this approach has been challenged recently because it is often felt that three suppliers simply are not enough to find out adequately what the market has to offer. Many buyers therefore use many more than three suppliers. Some organisations have policies of, for example, sending an RFQ to three suppliers for small items, to six suppliers for larger items and to every supplier they can find for major pieces of equipment. Additionally there is the **open tendering** method, used particularly in the public sector, where the buyer advertises in newspapers, magazines or online, and interested suppliers contact them to obtain details against which they can provide a quotation. It is difficult to give reasons for not using the RFQ system for new purchases so, if you do not use it, it could be that you only buy regularly used items from tried and tested suppliers.

Feedback on self-assessment question 12.3

You should make the point that RFQs should be sent to as many suppliers as is necessary to provide a reasonably full picture of what the supply market has to offer. There is no stipulation about the exact number of suppliers who should be so contacted, but three would be an absolute minimum. You may recommend that the number of suppliers who will be invited to quote should increase with the value of the order.

Feedback on learning activity 12.4

It would be unusual to find an organisation where a tendering process or negotiation takes place before every contract is awarded. Most organisations reserve its use for larger, more important contracts, especially those for capital equipment, for important services or for the annual supply of goods. Some public sector organisations have a policy of not negotiating with suppliers at all, but award contracts solely as a result of a tendering exercise. Many organisations, particularly in the public sector, have different procedures for different contract values. Examples might be that:

- For order values under £100, no formal purchasing or tendering process takes place.
- For order values between £100 and £1,000, three suppliers are requested to provide quotations.

- For order values over £1,000, a full tendering process involving all known suppliers will take place.

Feedback on self-assessment question 12.4

The answer is rather subjective. The fact is that *all* of these skills are important to a greater or lesser extent. The problem is that not everyone possesses all of them, and the important thing is to use well the ones you *do* have and try to develop the ones where you are lacking.

Many people would regard communication skills, both verbal and non-verbal, as being the most important, coupled perhaps with the ability to remain calm and rational.

Feedback on learning activity 12.5

The usual criteria would be:

- Price: is the supplier the lowest priced one of those approached at the RFQ stage?
- Delivery: how often, if at all, has the supplier delivered late?
- Quality: how many of the supplier's consignments been rejected on quality grounds?

Some organisations add other criteria such as:

- ease of obtaining information
- promptness and accuracy of documents
- reaction to being informed of problems.

If you do not have a formal vendor rating system it could be because you have only a few suppliers, whose performance can be monitored unofficially, or because your organisation believes that such a system is too costly in terms of time and effort.

Feedback on self-assessment question 12.5

Essentially the answer to this is that, if you have a formal vendor rating system, you can use it to find any data you need about suppliers' performance. Thus if, as you suppose, the suppliers are providing good service, the vendor rating system will demonstrate this.

12

Identification and evaluation of supply sources

You wouldn't want
to live with your
suppliers but you
can't live *without*
them.

Introduction

In this study session we shall consider the important purchasing task of making sure we have the right supplier *before* we take the risk of placing orders with them. This process, usually known as 'supplier appraisal' or 'supplier evaluation', involves finding out all we can about potential suppliers *before* we award contracts to them.

Session learning objectives

After completing this session you should be able to:

13.1 Identify different sources of information on potential suppliers.
13.2 Describe different methods of obtaining information on potential suppliers.
13.3 State the kinds of information required about potential suppliers.

Unit content coverage

This study session covers the following topics from the official CIPS unit content document:

Learning outcome

Describe the different approaches for verifying supplier information.

13

Learning objective

3.2 Identify potential sources of supply and obtain information on their capabilities. Methods to be used:
- Internet
- Networking
- Trade fairs and exhibitions
- Visits from company representatives
- Explain the pre-qualification criteria for new suppliers.
- Financial status
- Capacity of the company to produce
- Technical capability

Prior knowledge

Study session 12.

Resources

None specific but sound knowledge of your company's procedures would be useful, as would access to the internet.

Timing

You should set aside about 2 hours to read and complete this session, including learning activities, self-assessment questions, the suggested further reading (if any) and the revision question.

13.1 Sources of information on potential suppliers

Introduction

When we need to purchase something, either a product or service that we have never purchased before or one that we need to re-source, possibly because the existing supplier has ceased to be a 'good' supplier, the first task is to find a suitable supplier. To do this we need to find information on potential suppliers – in other words, companies that are in the business of supplying the type of goods and/or service that we want.

Information sources

You will have seen some of these in study session 12. Here we shall look at these in more detail and also consider some others.

- **Supplier catalogue**: a particularly useful means of finding suppliers. Catalogues are usually quick and easy to use, and suppliers are willing to send copies. Order and payment details are included in the catalogues.
- **Trade registers and directories**: organisations such as Dun & Bradstreet and Kelly's provide directories of suppliers. These generally provide information about suppliers' products or services and sometimes information on the financial and commercial capabilities of the supplier organisations. They are usually indexed alphabetically and by commodity.
- **Trade journals/trade association journals**: magazines such as *Supply Management*, or *Materials Handling News* usually include details and/or advertisements for companies operating in areas of commerce or industry that are relevant to the magazine's readership.
- **Trade exhibitions**: these can be a cost-effective means of sourcing and can allow the buyer:
  - to see new products and services, usually under a particular heading, for example warehousing equipment
  - to make contact with the sales people for each organisation
  - to discuss the products and services with the suppliers
  - to expand their knowledge and awareness of products and services of different suppliers.
- **Direct mail**: often 'binned', this information *can* be saved and accessed when required.
- **Sales representatives**: potentially useful but biased.
- **Internet**: you will be able to find information about literally thousands of suppliers on the internet. The only real problem is

that of information overload. However, as well as finding basic information such as the name and address of the company and the products/services supplied, you can send RFQs and other documents to them electronically.

Learning activity 13.1

Select a product or service that you currently purchase and assume it needs to be re-sourced. Use the internet to identify possible sources and record your experiences. For example, have many potential sources been identified? Does it appear that they might be satisfactory?

Think about whether you would normally use (for example) trade directories or your departmental records or any other information source. Note down any improvements otherwise that you believe the internet gives you.

Feedback on page 130

13.2 Obtaining information on potential suppliers

Having identified companies that are in the business of supplying the type of goods and services that we want, we now turn our attention to finding out information about these companies. This is so that, if we award contracts to them, we can be reasonably sure that they will be 'good' suppliers in terms of quality, price and service. There are several ways of doing this.

This process is known as 'supplier appraisal', 'supplier evaluation' or 'supplier quality assessment'. Some companies have a policy that orders will not be placed with a 'new' supplier until supplier appraisal has been satisfactorily performed. Some buyers tend to limit considerations to quality, but in reality all aspects of supplier performance should be covered.

Methods of carrying out supplier appraisal include the following:

- **Questionnaire**: a detailed questionnaire should be sent to the potential supplier. Answers can later be verified by visit.

Learning activity 13.2

Try to develop a questionnaire for obtaining information on potential suppliers. If your organisation already has one, see if you can improve it.

Feedback on page 130

- **Visit**: a potential supplier should be visited by a small team, including the buyer, quality manager, technical representative and/or any other

13

person from a background deemed relevant to the situation (the actual make-up of the team may change from potential supplier to potential supplier). The team should ask questions and draw inferences as to the likely performance of the potential supplier.

- **Reputation**: asking other buyers, trade associations, bank, etc.
- **Find out if the company is 'approved'**: by such bodies as the Ministry of Defence, British Aerospace, and so on (companies *must* be good to be approved suppliers of such bodies). Third-party accreditation (for example ISO 9000 series) should be examined also, and, increasingly, environmental accreditation such as ISO 14000 is considered important.

Self-assessment question 13.1

Draft a memorandum to your subordinates to explain why potential suppliers should be thoroughly appraised before you place orders with them.

Feedback on page 131

13.3 Information required about potential suppliers

In section 13.2 above we considered how to appraise a potential supplier. Here we shall consider some of the ways in which we can judge a supplier's capabilities irrespective of how we actually gain the information.

How to judge a potential supplier

This involves considerations of the following aspects.

- **Technical ability**: Can the company do the kind of work that you would be giving them? You can test this from their work-in-progress or in the case of service providers by following up references.
- **Production facilities**: Is the plant modern? Is it well maintained? Do they have planned maintenance? What is their capacity?

Learning activity 13.3

Write notes on the implications for the potential supplier's performance if the answer to these supplier appraisal questions is 'yes', and the implications if it is 'no'.

1   (a) Can the company carry out the kind of work that you would be giving them?
(b) Is the plant modern?
(c) Is it well maintained?
(d) Do they have planned maintenance?

(continued on next page)

Learning activity 13.3 *(continued)*

2 What would be the implication if the supplier's capacity was used up?

Feedback on page 131

- **Quality control**: are they approved by the kind of organisation mentioned earlier? Do they have 'accreditation' and 'proper' quality management systems?
- **Production control**: do they have systems to control production or is it merely haphazard?
- **Financial stability**: it is important to be sure that a potential supplier is financially stable because you do not want the company to go bankrupt once you have confirmed an important long-term contract with it, otherwise you will be 'back to square one'. Information can be gained from the following sources:
  - balance sheets (must be published by a public company, by law)
  - Dun & Bradstreet
  - 'the old boy network'.
- **Management ability**: important to the performance of any company. This can be gauged from morale and general 'housekeeping'. What lines of communication are there?

Self-assessment question 13.2

So far, we have assumed that potential suppliers that we want to appraise are in our own country. You may want to award a large contract to a company that is located in the Far East if they appear to be a 'good' supplier. Write notes on why appraising such a supplier is likely to be difficult, and how you would go about it.

Feedback on page 132

13

Revision question

Now try the revision question for this session on page 197.

Summary

In this study session we have examined the steps that buyers need to take before awarding contracts with suppliers. This involves, first, finding out about what suppliers exist in the supply market. This can be achieved by searching various sources of information such as:

- the internet
- purchase department records
- trade directories.

Once we know which companies *may* be able to satisfy our needs, the next step is to make as sure as possible that we shall award contracts only to sound, good quality suppliers. The way in which we do this is known as supplier appraisal and involves gathering as much information as we can about potential suppliers by sending them questionnaires, visiting them, following up references, and so on.

Suggested further reading

You might like to read about this subject in more detail in chapter 11 of Lysons and Farrington (2006).

Feedback on learning activities and self-assessment questions

Feedback on learning activity 13.1

You will, no doubt, be familiar with the internet and the need to search the world wide web using 'search engines'. If you entered a product or service it is likely that you will have seen literally hundreds of possible suppliers, although this depends on how obscure or otherwise the product or service is. Each supplier's website will probably give you plenty of detail about prices and so on.

You might find many overseas suppliers, and the information presented on the internet might be very fast and easy to access. You might find that the websites do not answer questions that you might have, or might give you too much or not enough detail, and you might find yourself 'overburdened' with possible suppliers. You might also find that suppliers found through 'traditional' means are easier to contact if you have questions to ask.

Feedback on learning activity 13.2

There is certainly no prescribed answer to this but the following might serve as a useful, if formal and rather detailed, model:

13

SUPPLIER APPRAISAL

Company name:
Company address:
Telephone number: Fax number:
Details of principal management (where applicable)
Managing Director:
Sales contact: Name:
Title:
Technical contact: Name:
Title:
Authorised representative regarding quality matters:
Name:
Title:

1	Are all products supplied manufactured under a quality management system that is independently assessed (for example, ISO 9002: EN 29002, MOD, etc)?	yes/no
2	Is there a company quality manual?	yes/no
3	Do you have a system with written procedures for:	
	(a) Quality assurance	yes/no
	(b) Manufacturing	yes/no
	(c) Procurement of materials	yes/no
4	Does this system conform to any other recognised standard?	yes/no

If yes, please enclose details.

5   Can you supply certificates of conformity if requested?   yes/no
    If the answer is yes, then please enclose a copy.
6   (a) Do you have a system for identifying and investigating the cause of quality
        problems?
    (b) Do you have a system to initiate corrective action?   yes/no
                                                                                                yes/no
7   Is quality assurance independent of production management?   yes/no
8   Do you use quality control testing techniques for both:
    (a) your raw materials   yes/no
    (b) your products   yes/no
9   Does your quality assurance system work to written product specifications?   yes/no
10 Do you keep adequate records of all production processes for each production   yes/no
    run?
11 Does your relevant documentation allow traceability to all process and   yes/no
    manufacturing conditions from any product, back to the raw material?
12 How long do you keep production and quality records?
13 How often do you review the effectiveness of your quality system?
14 Would you allow access to review your company's quality assurance system?   yes/no
Thank you.

You might not have devised anything as formal as this but these are typical
questions that should be asked in a supplier questionnaire.

Feedback on self-assessment question 13.1

The 'key' here is that companies with which you have had no previous
dealings are very much a unknown quantity, and if you place orders with
them without carrying out rigorous supplier appraisal you are risking being
let down in terms of quality, either of product or service and delivery
service. The fact that a company has a good general reputation or satisfies
other customers is no guarantee that they would prove to be a good supplier
to you. Thus it is important to make sure for yourself that a potential
supplier is likely to be a good one.

Feedback on learning activity 13.3

1   (a) This might seem a strange question because you might ask yourself
    why you would be appraising a company that could not do the required
    work. However, it could be that the supplier is not used to performing
    work of the technical sophistication that you require, even though they
    supply products or services in the same general category.
    (b)–(d) If the plant is modern it shows that the company has invested
    in its future, which shows confidence and is a good thing. It also shows
    that they can provide the latest technology. However, lack of modern
    plant and machinery is not necessarily a bad thing, provided the plant is
    well maintained with (for example) demonstrable planned maintenance.
    Planned maintenance means less likelihood of breakdowns, and is
    evidence of good organisation. There is a problem, however: new
    plant may mean that the company has over-invested, and is about
    to go into liquidation; old plant may indicate lack of funds and that
    the company might go into liquidation! The need for experience to
    interpret such situations cannot be overstated here, and if you feel you
    lack the necessary experience it is best to work with more experienced
    colleagues as part of a team.

13

2   This one is difficult: if the supplier's capacity is used up it could mean that they are very busy because their work is so good that many customers give them large amounts of business. Alternatively, it could mean that they are inefficient. Experience would help you to judge which one it is! The problem is that a good company whose capacity is used up may struggle to provide the goods and services that you want when you want them, so care is needed.

Feedback on self-assessment question 13.2

The difficulty is simply the fact that the potential supplier is located on the other side of the world and that performing a full appraisal, including a visit, would be extremely time-consuming and costly.

This, however, should not mean that appraisal is not done. If the contract is of great importance and the supplier is likely to be important to your organisation, appraisal should be performed. If the annual value of the contract is likely to run into millions of pounds sterling, it is surely worth spending a few thousand pounds at the outset and taking a few days to satisfy yourself that the supplier will be satisfactory by visiting it with a small team.

Alternatively, if you are happy to leave the work to third parties, companies such as Société Générale de Surveillance (a Swiss company based in Geneva) will perform appraisals for a fee.

13

Documentation requirements for effective sourcing

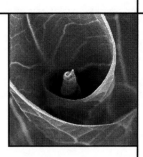

Good suppliers should be capable of anything (within reason!).

Introduction

In this study session we shall consider documentary requirements for sound purchasing. These include capability surveys, approved supplier lists and RFQs, which come in the early stages of the purchasing cycle (see study session 12). We shall then move on to vendor rating, which comes at the end of the purchasing cycle, and the types of documentation in the 'purchase to pay' process, which come in the middle of the purchasing cycle. We shall end by considering types of payment. In this way, we shall have covered all of the important types of documentation that can be applied at various stages of the purchasing cycle.

Session learning objectives

After completing this session you should be able to:

14.1 Demonstrate an ability to develop a capability survey document and an approved supplier list.
14.2 Present an example of a request for quotation.
14.3 Describe the process of vendor rating.
14.4 Distinguish between the various types of documentation in the purchase to pay processes.
14.5 State different forms of payment.

Unit content coverage

This study session covers the following topics from the official CIPS unit content document:

Learning outcome

Describe the different approaches for verifying supplier information.

Learning objective

3.3 Explain the pre-qualification criteria for new suppliers.
- Financial status
- Capacity of the company to produce
- Technical capability
- Adherence to systems and procedures
- Conformance to legislation
- The supplier's supply chain
- The supplier's customer base

14

- The culture of the company
- The identified costs of the proposed purchase

Prior knowledge

Study sessions 12 and 13.

Timing

You should set aside about 4 hours to read and complete this session, including learning activities, self-assessment questions, the suggested further reading (if any) and the revision question.

14.1 Capability surveys and approved supplier lists

These documents need to be developed in the early stages of the purchasing cycle. Capability surveys develop the work we did on supplier appraisal in study session 13 and require the buyer to find out more detailed information about a supplier's capabilities under these headings:

- technical/production
- financial
- commercial
- environmental.

Technical/production capabilities

In study study session 13 you will have seen an overview of the kind of issues that you need to consider under this heading when appraising new suppliers. Here, we shall look at this in more depth. Areas of their operation that you should be asking new suppliers questions about might be as follows:

- Capacity: maximum and current operating capacity in relation to their maximum.
- Research and development capability and proportion of turnover reinvested in R&D.
- Systems for managing quality such as ISO 9000.
- Implementation of total quality management.
- How non-conforming materials are dealt with.
- Inspection and testing procedures.
- Details of the equipment: output, efficiency, etc.
- How is the equipment maintained? Is there a planned maintenance programme?
- Does the supplier have a just-in time system?
- Use of mechanical/automated handling equipment.
- How is the workforce trained?
- Whether the workforce knows and understands the company's procedures for managing quality etc.

14

- How are inventories controlled for goods inwards/work in progress to finished output and delivery to the customer?

Financial capabilities

It is particularly important to appraise these when you are looking to develop a long-term relationship with a supplier. Capabilities in this area are important for suppliers to ensure supply continuity and reliability of quality and service. You may want to ask to see the supplier's accounts, including:

- Balance sheet: this tells you where the company's money is invested and where it came from, and will show the degree of risk associated with the money invested in the business.
- Profit and loss account: this shows how the business has grown or shrunk over time.
- Ratios are sometimes used to give a picture of such things as the supplier's cashflow position and profitability.

It is beyond our scope to examine such aspects in any detail here but you will look at them in much more depth elsewhere in your CIPS studies.

Commercial capabilities

A great deal of information about suppliers can be gleaned under this heading. This information can help paint a general picture of a supplier and give you an understanding of how they work and their commercial culture. 'Commercial capabilities' essentially refers to aspects of a supplier's operation that make them a good supplier to deal with on a day-to-day, week-to-week, basis. To get an idea of the kind of characteristics of a supplier that might come under this heading, proceed to learning activity 14.1 below.

Learning activity 14.1

See if you can put together a list of areas of information that you would like to have about new suppliers to give you a good general picture of how they operate in all respects. Warning: there is a lot of ground to cover!

Feedback on page 141

14

Environmental capabilities

Increasingly today, buyers need to be aware of and examine suppliers' environmental capabilities. Essentially, this is because your organisation cannot claim to be environmentally friendly if its suppliers, particularly major suppliers and supply chains, are not. The kind of areas you should cover in this respect are:

1   The recovery, recycling and reusing of materials and waste products.
2   The safe disposal of waste products that cannot be recycled.

3   Supplier selection policies to support firms that conform to environmental standards with regard to air, water and noise pollution.
4   Supplier and product selection policies that reflect concern for conservation and the renewal of resources.
5   The safe testing of products and materials.
6   Concern for noise, spray, dirt and vibration in the operation of transport facilities.

Self-assessment question 14.1

1   Do you agree with the view that purchasers should take an increasing concern of environmental issues?
2   Compose five separate questions you might ask a supplier if you were to appraise their environmental capabilities.

Feedback on page 141

14.2 Requests for quotation

Requests for quotation (RFQ) are also known as 'invitations to bid' and 'enquiries'.

We considered RFQ and the purpose behind them in study session 12. Here we shall look at the kind of information that you should give suppliers in an RFQ so that they may submit a suitable quotation.

Learning activity 14.2

Write down the kind of information that you believe should be found in a request for quotation.

Feedback on page 142

Drawings and specifications may accompany this enquiry form. Sufficient time should be allowed to enable the suppliers to prepare their quotations. In complex contracts, the period of time can be many months.

For larger contracts, many buyers select suppliers through competitive tender. The aim of a competitive tendering exercise is that a purchaser requests formal bids or tenders to be submitted by suppliers under conditions that will give all suppliers a fair and equal opportunity of winning a contract from the purchaser.

Competitive tendering usually involves procedures such as:

• All invitations to tender must be identical so individual suppliers or tenderers must not be offered different terms or information.

14

- Tenders will generally be kept secure until a set time of opening, for example Monday 19 December, 10.00 am.
- The tenders are usually opened by a representative of the procurement function and will generally be witnessed by another person.

The aim of a tendering process is to select the bid proposal that represents the best overall *value for money* by a balance between the five rights of quality, delivery, place, quantity and cost. It is important to consider the *total acquisition costs* of the tenders or quotations received, as the lowest price may not necessarily provide the best value.

Tendering promotes competition between suppliers as a way of improving the purchaser's ability to secure the best value for money.

Self-assessment question 14.2

You have been requested to purchase a quantity of eight desks of two different types:

- three 1600mm width
- five 1400mm width.

The user has developed specifications and requires the desks to be delivered within three weeks.

You are required to evaluate the quotations received and present recommendations for the award of the contract based on the following information:

	Supplier 1	Supplier 2	Supplier 3
1600mm desks	£75.70 each	£87.80 each	£93.00 each
1400mm desks	£60.60 each	£61.90 each	£72.00 each
Delivery			
1600mm desks	2 weeks	1 week	1 week
1400mm desks	4 weeks	1 week	1 week

In addition, Supplier 2 requires payment in 30 days and has a delivery charge of £5 per item. Supplier 3 offers 10% discount for payment within 14 days of delivery, and delivery charges are included in the unit prices. Supplier 1 requires payment within 60 days and requires a delivery charge of £50 per delivery.

You may assume that all three suppliers have been fully assessed and found acceptable, and that the items offered comply with the specification. The quality and appearance of the desks are equal. Price, delivery and payment are therefore the criteria that will distinguish the suppliers.

Feedback on page 142

14

14.3 Vendor rating

Supplier performance will generally be monitored by some form of vendor rating, which, as with vendor appraisal, may be carried out systematically, possibly through a computerised system, but could equally be a manual record maintained by individual purchasers on suppliers within their area of responsibility. Performance criteria to be monitored would normally include the following:

- Quality: defects, performance to specification, returns from customers.
- Price: changes, competitiveness.
- Delivery: on time, correct quantity.
- Administration: errors on delivery notes or invoices.

Learning activity 14.3

Write notes on how you would go about measuring these performance criteria in practice. If your initial response is to say that a computer would do it, remember that the computer needs to be given a formula to work on.

Feedback on page 143

Many buyers find that these 'objective' criteria are enough, but others feel that there are also more qualitative factors that should be taken into account to obtain a greater all-round picture of the supplier and its performance.

It is important that you keep suppliers informed of their ratings. In addition to information on their own performance, you may wish to provide suppliers with league tables ranking suppliers showing their position, but not identifying other suppliers, for reasons of confidentiality. You also need to hold regular meetings between buyers, users and suppliers to provide feedback on performance and to identify changes in order to bring about improvements. These should be discussed with the supplier and incorporated in supplier development programmes.

14

Self-assessment question 14.3

As a buyer you feel that objective criteria such as we have considered are not far reaching enough to provide adequate measurement of suppliers. Write a list of other criteria that you would like to be included in a vendor rating system to provider a fuller supplier picture.

Feedback on page 143

14.4 Documentation in the purchase-to-pay process

This section examines the various documents that accompany and record the 'purchase-to-pay' process: in other words, the process from placing the purchase order with a supplier to settling the invoice relating to the order.

These documents, in order, are:

- Purchase order: this is the document whereby the purchaser informs the seller of what they would like to purchase, often because of a tendering process (see section 14.2 above), along with other important reference information. It will usually be preceded by a purchase requisition (see study session 12).

Learning activity 14.4

Note down what information you believe a purchase order should contain.

Feedback on page 143

- Acknowledgement: returned by the supplier to the buyer to confirm receipt of the order. Buyers sometimes ignore the acknowledgement but, as you will see in study sessions 17 and 18, it can have important legal consequences. It should agree with the purchase order in every detail.
- Advice note: this is a note sent by the supplier to the buyer indicating that delivery of the goods is in the process of being arranged. It allows the purchaser's goods inward and stores departments to prepare for receiving the goods.
- Packing note: often a copy of the advice note accompanying the consignment.
- Goods received note (GRN): a document completed by the goods inward department to indicate to the buying and accounts payable departments that the goods have arrived satisfactorily. Any shortages or damage to goods identified on arrival should be noted.
- Invoice: sent by the supplier to the purchaser as a request for payment. Provided it agrees with the order and GRN it should be settled within the required payment period. If it does not agree with these documents, it should be queried with the supplier.

14

Self-assessment question 14.4

1   It is important that, on each document, references to the other documents should be made. Explain why this should be.
2   The whole process described above may be performed electronically, as many organisations do today. In this event, what safeguards should be used?
3   Some organisations do not check or query invoices under a certain value (for example, £100.00). Some use an electronic system for automatic invoice checking and payment and build in a 'tolerance' so that, for example, if the invoice figure is within £50.00 of the purchase order figure the system will not query it. Explain why these two instances of 'not checking/querying' might be allowed to happen.

Feedback on page 144

14.5 Payment methods

Once all of the documents referred to in section 14.4 above have been reconciled so that the invoice tallies with the purchase order and GRN, the invoice should be paid promptly, in full. You should remember that late payment *might* mean that you incur interest charges, and it will certainly adversely affect the relationship you have with the supplier. Remember also that some suppliers offer extra discount for early payment.

Learning activity 14.5

What is the standard payment method used at your company? Does it present any problems? Are there any other suitable methods that could be used?

Feedback on page 144

One method of paying suppliers is by the use of corporate credit cards. Now attempt this:

Self-assessment question 14.5

Write a report of no more than 200 words to colleagues and management outlining what you believe to be the advantages and disadvantages of credit card payments. Include any safeguards that you feel should be included to minimise disadvantages.

Feedback on page 144

14

Revision question

Now try the revision question for this session on page 197.

Summary

In this study session we have considered:

- Aspects of the process of finding out, by means of a capability survey, what suppliers for the products and services that we need exist in the market.
- Finding out by means of an RFQ whether individual companies are able to supply us with what we need and if so, at what price and other details.
- How to monitor the performance of suppliers to which we have awarded contracts.

- What documentation processes should be in place to control the supply process.
- How to pay suppliers.

Suggested further reading

You may like to read about these subjects in more detail in chapters 11 and 16 of Lysons and Farrington (2006).

Feedback on learning activities and self-assessment questions

Feedback on learning activity 14.1

This list is fairly comprehensive, so do not worry if you did not get all of the points. But these are the kind of areas that you need to consider when looking at a new supplier's capabilities.

- When the company was established: how long in its present business.
- If the company is an autonomous concern or part of a larger group.
- The company's product or service range.
- The maximum and minimum contract values the supplier is willing to undertake.
- The company's development over the past few years.
- Key personnel (sales account manager, managing director, etc).
- Locations.
- Address, phone, fax numbers, email address, etc.
- Lead times for the product range.
- Other customers with contact addresses.
- How a customer order is processed.
- Use of computer systems in operations management.
- Whether the company makes to order or to stock.
- Choice of distribution channel.
- Ability and willingness to give cost breakdown.
- Structure of the organisation in a chart.
- Percentage of business for export/domestic markets.
- Preferred currency for payment.
- Details of the supplier's purchasing.

Feedback on self-assessment question 14.1

1 Your answer should be 'yes'. Environmental issues should be of an increasing concern to all organisations. Professional purchasers need to demonstrate that they have sourced from environmentally friendly suppliers. Sometimes buying environmentally friendly goods or services may appear to involve paying over the odds. You might sometimes have to make a business case to, for example, shareholders concerned about the return on their investment that doing this would enhance the view of your organisation in its own markets.

2 Wording is not important, but any five from these would suffice:
   (a) How are you attempting to recover, recycle or reuse materials and waste products in your production process?

14

(b) How do you safely dispose of waste products that cannot be recycled?

(c) Do you have, or are you planning to implement, a supplier selection policy to support firms that conform to environmental standards with regard to air, water and noise pollution?

(d) Do you have, or are you planning to implement, a supplier selection policy to support firms that reflect concern for conservation and the renewal of resources?

(e) How do you conduct the testing of products and materials in a manner that is safe to the environment?

(f) How do you show concern for noise, spray, dirt and vibration in the operation of transport facilities?

Feedback on learning activity 14.2

Again, there is quite a list here, but each of these is important:

- The title ('request for quotation', or similar). This might seem obvious and will probably be part of the document template but it is important so that suppliers cannot claim that they thought it was an order.
- Name, address and contact details of the purchaser.
- Name and address of supplier.
- Date.
- Purchaser's reference – again, probably part of the document template but aids the audit trail.
- Quantity required.
- Description of goods/service required.
- Required delivery place(s).
- Space for supplier to indicate prices.
- Requisition reference: again, to aid the audit trail
- Contractual terms: we shall consider these in study sessions 16 – 20.

Your organisation might have other pieces of information that you could include.

Feedback on self-assessment question 14.2

It is usually helpful to present the results of the evaluation in a matrix so that all the information relevant to the evaluation can be compared more easily.

	Supplier 1	Supplier 2	Supplier 3
1600mm desks (3)	£227.10	£263.40	£279.00
1400mm desks (5)	£303.00	£309.50	£360.00
Total	£530.10	£572.90	£639.00
Delivery	2 weeks (1600mm) 4 weeks (1400mm)	1 week	1 week
Charges	£100 (2 × £50)	£40 (8 × £5)	Included
Payment	60 days	30 days	10% discount within 14 days
Total cost	£630.10	£612.90	£575.10

Supplier 1 is rejected because it cannot meet the specified delivery requirement of within 3 weeks. Suppliers 2 and 3 meet the delivery requirements, but the early payment discount offered by Supplier 3 results in a lower price.

Supplier 3 should therefore be selected, unless the accounts department is unable to meet a 14 day payment, in which case Supplier 2 would be preferred.

Feedback on learning activity 14.3

You may have thought of something different, but the usual ways of measuring these criteria are:

- Quality: measure the number or percentage of defects over a period of time.
- Price: was the supplier the lowest bidder at the tendering stage (meaning that it is competitive), or how many price increases have been requested in (for example) the past 12 months and how great have they been?
- Delivery: measure the number or percentage of late deliveries from the supplier.
- Administration: measure the number of errors, for example invoices showing the wrong price or presented far too early.

Feedback on self-assessment question 14.3

A typical list of criteria might be:

- after-sales service
- willingness to become involved in design, cost reduction, etc
- investment programmes
- good communication
- flexibility and proposing good ideas
- efficient paperwork.

These criteria may be weighted, depending on their perceived importance, and each supplier scored against each criterion to produce an overall score, although not all will be relevant to every purchasing situation.

Feedback on learning activity 14.4

Such information might vary from organisation to organisation, but an order *should* contain:

- Purchase order number.
- Date.
- Purchaser's requisition number (for reference purposes).
- Supplier's name and address (obviously!).
- Purchaser's address and delivery location(s).
- Purchaser's name, invoice address (it might be different from the delivery address) and account code.
- Quantity, full description and price of the goods. The price should have been agreed beforehand: *never* put 'to be advised', or similar; you are giving the supplier carte blanche to charge any amount they want.

14

- Any codes required such as product codes.
- Name, telephone, fax and email details of buyer for contact purposes.
- Terms and conditions of contract (usually on the reverse).

You may have been able to think of some others.

Feedback on self-assessment question 14.4

1   The purpose of references on the documents is for cross-referencing purposes so that there is a complete and unbroken audit trail. This is so that, if you have one document, for example a GRN, a reference on this *should* give you access to all of the other documents so that all may be reconciled.

2   The important thing is that all electronic versions of the documents have the same cross-referencing information as paper versions. This is without discussing such issues as 'e-security', which is beyond our scope here.

3   The reason for this apparent 'sloppiness' or lack of control is that it would cost far more to follow up the queries than merely to allow the invoices to be settled, particularly in large organisations with complex processes/systems.

Feedback on learning activity 14.5

Specific feedback is impossible because of the nature of the activity, but the standard payment method used today is credit transfer. A problem might be that, because it tends to have standard payment days (for example the 26th of the month), it might mean that you are unable to receive early payment discounts. Increasingly, companies use corporate credit cards. Other payment methods include cheques and petty cash although both, particularly the latter, are seldom used today.

Feedback on self-assessment question 14.5

The advantages are that it allows routine purchases to be performed by non-purchasing staff, allowing them to get on with more important activities such as negotiating important contracts. This reduces the amount of invoicing (and other) administration required.

The disadvantages are that it can lead to inappropriate purchases being made by staff without sufficient authority from suppliers who do not give the best deal. Also, it can lead to purchases being made for items that are, in fact, covered by a 'blanket order', leading to extra administration and the advantages of the blanket order, such as large quantity discount, being lost.

Safeguards are that only authorised staff can use the credit card for purchases within a certain limit (for example £500) for authorised products or services from authorised suppliers. Also, authorised suppliers should be instructed to refuse attempted purchases that do not conform to the above conditions.

14

Study session 15
Verification of suppliers' capabilities

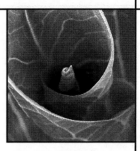

Suppliers should be capable of anything you want – shouldn't they?

Introduction

In previous study sessions we have introduced the process of supplier appraisal. In this study session we shall continue with this theme and examine how we might obtain more detailed appraisal and evaluation of potential supply sources, with particular reference to 'behind the scenes' work such as financial appraisal.

Session learning objectives

After completing this session you should be able to:

15.1 Describe how to follow up suppliers' references.
15.2 Explain how to carry out a financial assessment of a supplier.
15.3 Identify specific aspects of supplier performance including their ability to manage high volumes and delivery, and quality records.

Unit content coverage

This study session covers the following topics from the official CIPS unit content document:

Learning outcome

Describe the different approaches for verifying supplier information.

Learning objective

3.4 Identify the different ways of verifying the information provided by suppliers including:
 • References
 • Financial assessments
 • Ability to manage high volumes
 • Delivery and quality records

Prior knowledge

Study sessions 13 and 14.

Resources

None specific although a sound knowledge of your workplace procedures would be useful.

15

145

Timing

You should set aside about 2½ hours to read and complete this session, including learning activities, self-assessment questions, the suggested further reading (if any) and the revision question.

15.1 Following up suppliers' references

In study sessions 13 and 14 we examined the process of supplier appraisal or evaluation. One of the ideas mentioned there was that of obtaining references from potential suppliers. This involves asking potential suppliers for contact details of some of their customers so that you can ask these customers what they think of the supplier and what their experiences have been. The idea is very similar to a prospective employer asking a job candidate for references of their past employment.

One potential drawback with asking potential suppliers for customer references is that you will be directed only to customers with whom the supplier has a good relationship, so that you are unlikely to get any negative answers. Consequently, you might feel that you are unlikely to obtain a 'rounded' picture of the supplier. This can be offset largely by asking the supplier for a customer list so that *you* can choose which customers you contact. If a potential supplier refuses to provide such a list you should be wary of dealing with them and at least ask why they are unwilling to provide this information. It is not unreasonable to take the view that, if they do refuse to provide references, they must have something to hide. Beware!

Learning activity 15.1

If you were following up a potential supplier's references, what questions would you want to ask the 'referee'? Note down your answers and check them with the text that follows.

Feedback on page 154

The purpose of following up references is to obtain an unbiased view of a potential supplier's performance to give you an idea of how they are likely to behave towards you and your organisation. To this end, *any* question that you feel is relevant is fair but, typically, questions about the supplier to the 'referee' might include the following:

- How would you rate their quality?
- How consistent is their quality? Please give any examples of poor quality.
- How would you rate their service?
- How consistent is their service? (Please give examples, as above.)
- How do you measure quality and service?
- How flexible are they in terms of delivery or specification changes, even at short notice?
- How willing are they to contribute to specifications at the development stage?

15

- Have they made you aware of innovations?
- How responsive are they to queries and/or complaints?
- How easy is it to obtain information from them?

Alongside this process of following up customer references it can be useful to find out whether the supplier is accredited to BS EN ISO 9000: 2000 (or any part of it). This is beyond our scope here, but accreditation gives an unbiased view of a supplier's management structure, resource management, production processes and how they measure and improve their product and processes.

If your organisation is particularly keen to display its environmental credentials and/or is accredited itself to ISO 14000, it is important to try to select suppliers that are similarly accredited.

Self-assessment question 15.1

You have followed up some customer references and the information you have gained is that the supplier that is the subject of the references has been late with delivery on 5% of occasions and has had deliveries rejected on quality grounds on 8% of occasions. What further information might you need to be able to make a decision about whether the supplier is one you would want to deal with?

Feedback on page 154

15.2 Carrying out a financial assessment of a supplier

A supplier's financial capabilities should be appraised before you buy from it, particularly when you are looking to develop a long-term relationship with a supplier. Financial capability is essential for suppliers to ensure continuity of supply and reliability of product/service quality. To gain this information you can ask to see copies of the supplier's accounts. These *must* be published by law in the case of limited companies, but you should be suspicious of other companies not being willing to share such information with you.

It is impossible to provide a thorough review of accounting here, but the basics are as follows:

Balance sheet

This tells us where a company's money is invested and where it came from. It comprises:

- Assets: where the money has been invested, comprising
  - fixed assets: long-term investments such as land, buildings and machinery
  - current assets: short-term investments such as stocks and cash.
- Liabilities: sources of the company's finances, which can be either short term or long term.

The balance sheet provides a 'snapshot' of the company's financial situation at any given time.

15

Here is an example. All the figures quoted are in thousands of pounds. The three noughts are missed off to make the accounts easier to read.

Balance sheet ABC Ltd	2003	2004	2005
Fixed assets:			
Property	400	845	1,325
Plant and equipment	1,200	1,350	2,250
	1,600	2,195	3,575
Current assets:			
Stock	1,000	1,050	1,450
Debtors (money owed by the supplier's customers)	1,400	1,300	1,850
Cash	50	250	–
	2,450	2,600	3,300
Total net assets (fixed assets + current assets)	4,050	4,795	6,875
Current liabilities:			
Creditors (money owed to suppliers)	1,100	1,400	1,600
Tax owing (money owed to government)	270	250	230
Dividends owing (profits distributed to shareholders in proportion to shares held in the business)	100	120	60
Bank overdraft (short-term debt owed to banks)	–	–	900
	1,470	1,770	2,790
Net current assets (total net assets – current liabilities)	980	830	510
Total assets (fixed assets + net current assets)	2,580	3,025	4,085
Less long-term loans	400	500	1,100
Net total assets	2,180	2,525	2,985
Financed by:			
Share capital (money invested by shareholders)	800	1,000	1,300
Reserves (balance on profit and loss account – trading profit reinvested in the business)	1,380	1,525	1,685
Total	2,180	2,525	2,985

Learning activity 15.2

Assets *should* always equal liabilities, hence the term 'balance sheet'. Make sure that the balance sheet above does actually balance by adding up the assets and the liabilities.

Feedback on page 155

15

Profit and loss account

This shows how the business has grown or shrunk over a period of time. Let us consider an example from the same company as before, ABC. Again, all the figures quoted are in £000s.

Profit and loss statement ABC Ltd	2003	2004	2005
Turnover (sales revenue)	6,100	6,500	6,750
Cost of sales (costs of production)	5,400	5,850	6,025
Gross profit	700	650	725
Selling, distribution and administration expenses	60	75	95
Profit before interest and taxation	640	575	630
Interest payable	45	68	76
Taxation payable	270	250	230
Profit after interest and taxation	325	257	324
Dividends	125	112	164
Reserves (retained profit for the year)	200	145	160

Turnover or sales is the revenue that the company will have earned from their trading activities, and will normally be net (after) of any returns, discounts allowed, or commission paid to agents, etc.

From this figure, the gross profit is calculated by subtracting the cost of sales. The cost of sales figure will take into account their production costs and purchases from their suppliers over the year.

The selling, distribution and administration overheads, such as the wages and salaries of these functional areas, their advertising and promotional expenses, telephone, postage, travel, stationery costs etc, are then subtracted from the *gross profit*.

The *profit before interest and taxation* is a very significant profit figure – as there are several 'levels' of profit listed in the profit and loss account – because it can be interpreted as the profit arising out of the actual trading operations of the business. From this, the financing costs in terms of loan interest (usually the cost of loans from banks) are deducted, as is the tax on ordinary activities.

Finally, the dividends are deducted, and these are the share of profit after tax that the company's shareholders decide to take out of the business as a return on their investment in the company to leave retained profit or reserves.

In conducting a financial appraisal of a supplier, ratios are often provided as a summary statistic. These help show trends over time in terms of the viability and performance of the supplier. There are several important ratios:

Profitability:

$$\text{Profit margin} = \frac{\text{Profit before interest and tax}}{\text{Sales revenue (turnover)}} \times 100$$

$$\text{Profitability} = \frac{\text{Profit before interest and tax}}{\text{Total assets}} \times 100$$

$$\text{Return on capital employed} = \frac{\text{Profit before interest and tax}}{\text{Capital employed}} \times 100$$

(Capital employed = shareholders' funds + long-term loans)

Liquidity:

$$\text{Current ratio} = \frac{\text{Current assets}}{\text{Current liabilities}}$$

$$\text{Acid or quick ratio} = \frac{\text{Current assets less stock}}{\text{Current liabilities}}$$

$$\text{Stock turnover} = \frac{\text{Cost of sales}}{\text{Stock}}$$

$$\text{Credit period} = \frac{\text{Debtors}}{\text{Sales revenue}} \times 365 \text{ days}$$

Gearing:

$$\text{Gearing} = \frac{\text{Long-term loans}}{\text{Shareholders' funds}}$$

Financial markets:

$$\text{Return on shareholders' funds} = \frac{\text{Profit after interest and tax}}{\text{Shareholders' funds}} \times 100$$

The first category is the *profitability* ratios. These measure the performance of the supplier in terms of their ability to exceed costs and make a profit. Any company has to generate sufficient revenue from their trading operations to cover all of their costs, pay a dividend to their shareholders as a return on the money they have invested in the company, and then have some profit left over to plough back into the business as reserves.

The second area is *liquidity*. These can be straightforward ratios to calculate and are a measure of the cashflow position of the supplier. The *current ratio* measures the relationship between a company's immediate or short-term debts (current liabilities) and the value of their current assets out of which these debts will have to be paid. The *acid* or *quick ratio* is a prime measure of a company's liquidity, of its ability to meet short-term debts as it assumes that stocks (inventories) cannot necessarily be readily converted into money. The *credit period* measures the average number of days it takes for the supplier to collect their payments owed from customers (other purchasing organisations). It can reveal how quickly the supplier may want to be paid.

The third category is *gearing*. This is the proportion of a company's funding that is represented by long-term loans. A company that is highly geared is susceptible to increases in their financing costs, which could be brought about through an increase in interest rates.

Finally, financial markets may judge the company's performance on their *return on shareholders funds*. This is a measure of the return on investment that the shareholders have obtained on the capital they have invested in the company.

Ratios can provide a useful benchmark of the supplier, as these trends can be compared with the performance of other suppliers.

Self-assessment question 15.2

1 Calculate the ratios indicated below on the basis of the following balance sheet and profit and loss statements provided for each of the three years:

Balance sheet ABC Ltd	2003	2004	2005
Fixed assets:			
Property	400	845	1,325
Plant and equipment	1,200	1,350	2,250
Current assets:			
Stock	1,000	1,050	1,450
Debtors (money owed by the supplier's customers)	1,400	1,300	1,850
Cash	50	250	–
Current liabilities:			
Creditors (money owed to suppliers)	1,100	1,400	1,600
Tax owing (money owed to government)	270	250	230
Dividends owing (profits distributed to shareholders in proportion to shares held in the business)	100	120	60
Bank overdraft (short-term debt owed to banks)	–	–	900
Long-term liabilities:			
Long-term loans	400	500	1,100
Share capital (money invested by shareholders)	800	1,000	1,300
Reserves (balance on profit and loss account – trading profit reinvested in the business)	1,380	1,525	1,685

Profit and loss statement ABC Ltd	2003	2004	2005
Turnover (sales revenue)	6,100	6,500	6,750
Cost of sales (costs of production)	5,400	5,850	6,025
Gross profit (turnover – cost of sales)	700	650	725
Selling, distribution and administration expenses	60	75	95

(continued on next page)

Self-assessment question 15.2 *(continued)*

Profit and loss statement ABC Ltd	2003	2004	2005
Profit before interest and taxation	640	575	630
Interest payable	45	68	76
Taxation payable	270	250	230
Profit after interest and taxation	325	257	324
Dividends	125	112	164
Reserves (retained profit for the year)	200	145	160

Profitability

Profit margin =

Profitability =

Return on capital employed =

Liquidity

Current ratio =

Acid or quick ratio =

Stock turnover =

Credit period =

Gearing =

Financial markets

Return on shareholders' funds =

2   Try to identify what trends are revealed over the three-year period.

Feedback on page 155

15.3 Specific aspects of supplier performance

In previous study sessions we have considered the appraisal/evaluation of potential suppliers in terms of their ability to supply the right quality and quantity. There are some situations, however, where it is necessary to appraise suppliers' abilities in more depth to ensure that they are able to meet specific requirements. Such requirements might include the ability to manage high volumes or to provide innovative quality solutions.

High volumes

Sometimes buyers' quantity requirements might include the need to purchase volumes, often on a regular, recurring basis, that are beyond the normal expectations of suppliers. In this situation it is important that, as part of the appraisal process, this requirement is discussed with the potential supplier and evidence is submitted to support any such ability claimed by the supplier. It might also be necessary to follow this up with specific discussion with any customer references (see section 15.1 above) that you might follow up.

A similar situation is where required quantities might change greatly, either up or down, at short notice. Again, suppliers' ability to cope with such changes should be ascertained at the appraisal stage.

Learning activity 15.3

Think about quantity requirements in your workplace. If you have encountered situations where these either might be extremely large or are likely to be subject to frequent change, note down how you would ascertain suppliers' ability to cope with such situations.

Feedback on page 155

Innovation

You might look to suppliers to provide innovation on a regular, ongoing basis to improve your organisation's product or service. This is particularly true in a manufacturing environment where suppliers can contribute proactively to the ongoing development of the purchaser's product by looking to improve the design of the part or sub-assembly they are supplying. This process is known as early supplier involvement (ESI), and has been mentioned previously, particularly in section 9.3.

When you are buying services it is worth remembering that service providers should be able to provide advice as to how the service in question should be carried out.

Again, specific enquiry should be made about suppliers' abilities in such areas at the appraisal stage. *Any* specific, unusual, requirement that you might want from suppliers should be discussed in detail at the appraisal stage and, where necessary, followed up with reference to the supplier's customers.

15

Self-assessment question 15.3

Make a list of five 'unusual' aspects of supplier performance that you think should be appraised in addition to the 'normal' quality, capacity, service and so on. In answering, try to think about the modern commercial world and its requirements, and do not be afraid to ask colleagues for their suggestions.

Feedback on page 156

Revision question

Now try the revision question for this session on page 198.

Summary

In this study session we have extended the concept of supplier appraisal to cover:

- The importance of following up suppliers' customer references to obtain a more independent, unbiased, view of a supplier's capabilities.
- The use and value of financial data to ascertain a supplier's financial position, this being crucial to a supplier's ability to supply and continue to supply the goods or services that we require.
- The need to include any special or specific requirements in our supplier appraisal process.

Suggested further reading

You can read about this in more detail in chapter 11 of Lysons and Farrington (2006).

Feedback on learning activities and self-assessment questions

Feedback on learning activity 15.1

Feedback can be found in the text relating to this learning activity, but you should remember that such questions must be relevant to your particular situation and requirements. You may find that you would have to 'read between the lines' of the referee's answer because it is unlikely that a referee would openly criticise a supplier severely. Also, a supplier would not nominate a referee who would not give the 'right' answer, although this may be offset by the list approach.

Feedback on self-assessment question 15.1

The supplier in question is certainly not perfect, and if you are pursuing a 'zero defects' policy you might feel that it would be unsafe to buy from them at all. However, their record is not disastrous and it might be acceptable. Questions to the customers providing the references that might help you make a decision would be:

- Have any of the problems been your fault? Have you, for example, changed delivery times at short notice or changed specifications without the supplier's agreement?
- How serious were the problems? For example, were quality problems so severe that there were long delays in getting them resolved?
- How cooperative was the supplier in terms of rectifying the problems?
- How concerned did the supplier appear to be regarding the problems?

You might be able to think of others.

15

Feedback on learning activity 15.2

You should have worked out that assets and liabilities for each year are equal:

The figure for 2003 is £4,050,000; for 2004 it is £4,795,000; and for 2005 is £6,875,000.

Feedback on self-assessment question 15.2

1　The ratio figures are as follows:

	2003	2004	2005
Profitability			
Profit margin	10.49	8.85	9.33
Profitability	15.80	11.99	9.16
Return on capital employed	24.81	19	15.42
Liquidity			
Current ratio	1.67	1.47	1.18
Acid or quick ratio	0.99	0.87	0.66
Stock turnover	6.10	6.19	4.65
Credit period	83.77	73	100
Gearing	15.50	16.50	26.93
Financial markets			
Return on shareholders' funds	14.91	10.18	10.85

2　You may have been able to identify that the ratios show a worsening financial situation for ABC over the years 2003–2005. Generally, the following have all deteriorated over the period:
- the firm's profitability (the measure. of the supplier performance in terms of its ability to exceed costs and make a profit)
- liquidity (the measure of the relationship between a company's immediate or short-term debts (current liabilities) and the value of their current assets out of which these debts will have to be paid)
- gearing (the proportion of a company's funding that is represented by long-term loans)
- attractiveness to financial markets.

This information might make you very reticent to use this supplier because these trends are decidedly unhealthy!

Feedback on learning activity 15.3

Your answer should include discussing the matter with the supplier in the first instance. The confidence (or otherwise) shown by your contact in the supplier's organisation should be noted, and especially if this appears to be lacking you should seek evidence, either by asking to see the supplier's records of how they deal with customer orders or by asking customer 'referees'. If suppliers do not appear to have full records of customer orders and how they deal with them, you should be suspicious.

15

Feedback on self-assessment question 15.3

Your answer might include any five of the following:

- where potential suppliers do not hold BS EN ISO 9000:2000
- the purchase of non-standard items
- when entering into just-in-time (JIT) arrangements
- when considering global sourcing
- when considering the establishment of e-procurement arrangements with suppliers
- when negotiating outsourcing arrangements
- when negotiating service level agreements.

Additionally, you may have thought of some others.

The legal system

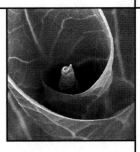

'Ignorance of the law excuses no man from practising it.'
Addison Mizner

Introduction

In this study session we shall begin to examine aspects of law that affect purchasing and supply, an examination that will occupy the rest of this unit. Law is a huge subject, and we shall do little more than 'scratch the surface'. However, it is very important, because every day buyers may enter into contracts or other dealings that might have legal consequences. Buyers often say that they do not need to study law because there are lawyers to deal with legal disputes, but if you know nothing of law:

- How do you know when you need to contact a lawyer?
- How would you understand what a lawyer was telling you?

In this study session we shall concern ourselves with the different types of law and law court that exist.

Session learning objectives

After completing this session you should be able to:

16.1 Distinguish between common law and statute law.
16.2 Distinguish between different types of court and between criminal law and civil law.
16.3 State the role of European law in the English legal system.

Unit content coverage

Learning outcome

Identify the essential elements of a legally binding agreement.

Learning objective

4.1 Provide an overview of the legal system, the sources of law:
- The basis of the legal system in the UK and in Europe
- The difference between statutes and case law
- The role of Parliament and the judiciary

16

Timing

You should set aside about 3 hours to read and complete this session, including learning activities, self-assessment questions, the suggested further reading (if any) and the revision question.

16.1 Differences between common law and statute law

How do laws come into existence? In Britain and in other common law countries, there are two main sources: **statutes** and **common law**.

Statutes

These become law by Acts of Parliament, but the decisions of judges also affect statute law. Very few statutes are written so clearly that it is easy to understand them, and in fact some are written so obscurely that it is very hard to understand them. Consequently several court cases have been about what phrases and sentences in particular Acts of Parliament mean, and how provisions of an Act are to be interpreted. The findings of the court are regarded as part of the law.

Also, circumstances change, technology and commerce develop, and questions arise as to how existing Acts apply in new conditions. If these questions are argued out in the law courts, the answers defined by the judges may also become part of the law. Such interpretations are known as 'case law' or 'judicial precedent' and will affect the outcome of future cases so that court decisions will be based on such precedent. The type of court in which the precedent is made dictates the importance attached to the precedent, so that a decision made in the Court of Appeal would outweigh a ruling made in a 'lesser' court such as the High Court (see section 16.2 below)

Statute law thus comprises all those Acts of Parliament currently in force, plus the case law that clarifies the meaning or the application of the Acts.

Learning activity 16.1

Several statutes affect purchasing and supply. Using research, for example on the internet (the CIPS website might be useful here) or by consulting your company lawyer or legal department, identify and summarise the main statutes that affect purchasing activities.

Feedback on page 163

It is beyond our scope here to discuss the above statutes in more depth but you will encounter them later in your CIPS studies.

Common law

This is assumed to exist already and to be known to everyone, but is affected, and in some cases changed, by the decisions of judges in cases under common law. It is often said that common law originated 'in the mists of time'. However, these days, it originates almost totally from case law and so is changing all the time, if only gradually, as a result of principles established by legal cases.

Common law provides the context for statute law. For instance, it states what a contract is. It also includes laws that are not explicitly stated in writing in the way that statutes are, but nevertheless are evidenced clearly enough by case law.

16

Self-assessment question 16.1

Write an essay of not more than 200 words explaining the differences between common law and statute law.

Feedback on page 163

16.2 Criminal law and civil law and different types of court

English law is divided into two main parts:

- **Criminal law** covers such crimes as murder, theft and road traffic offences. It also covers a few offences that have to do with purchasing transactions, such as breaches of the Trade Descriptions acts (1968 and 1972), which make it an offence to give a false trade description of goods or a false indication of price in the course of business or trade. Persons charged with offences under criminal law are called defendants. The person bringing the action is called the prosecutor. If defendants are found guilty they are punished by the court, usually by fines or imprisonment.
- **Civil law** is concerned not with punishment but with compensation. It includes contract law and the Sale of Goods Act, as well as other statutes that were mentioned in section 16.1, such as the Unfair Contract Terms Act. Actions (or 'suits') are usually brought by the aggrieved party, called the plaintiff (not the prosecutor), who sues (not prosecutes) the defendant. A plaintiff who wins the case will be compensated by the court in some way, usually by a sum of money to be paid by the defendant, known as damages, although other remedies are possible, and we shall examine some of these in study session 20.

You will note that we use the term 'English law' as opposed to 'British law'. This is because there is no such thing, strictly speaking, as British law: Scottish law has some significant differences from English law and must be treated separately.

This brings us to the different types of court that exist in Britain and their roles. These break down into:

- magistrates' court
- Crown Court
- county court
- High Court
- Court of Appeal.

16

Learning activity 16.2

Using the internet, or by talking to your company's legal representative, obtain an overview of the role of each of the above courts.

Feedback on page 163

Magistrates' court

This is a court of first instance (in which cases start) for *all* criminal cases of no matter what seriousness. Serious crime will be transferred, after initial investigation by the magistrates, to the Crown Court. Petty crime will be dealt with here by three lay magistrates appointed from the local community and advised on legal matters by the justices' clerk. Magistrates refer serious cases to the:

Crown Court

This is the highest court in which criminal trials take place. It has a judge and a jury of 12 persons, who are taken at random from the electoral roll. It has higher powers of sentence and hears appeals from the magistrates' courts. This court deals with all serious crimes, and it is possible to send convicted persons from the magistrates' to the Crown Court for sentence in cases where the justices feel their powers of sentence are inadequate.

Appeal from here lies automatically to the Court of Appeal Criminal Division in London.

County court

This is a first instance *civil* court. It hears all cases relating to contracts and other civil matters up to a value of £5,000 (£30,000 in the case of land, trusts and wills). These figures are correct at the time of writing (early 2006). Claims of higher values must go to the High Court.

It deals with mostly petty civil cases of debt, and personal accident cases. County courts, like magistrates' courts, are local and based in most towns.

Appeals from here do not go to the High Court but to the Court of Appeal Civil Division in London.

High Court

This is the main civil court in the system. It is divided into three parts:

- Family Division: handling divorce, matrimonial and children cases, ward of court actions and similar.
- Chancery Division: handling company and partnership actions, bankruptcy, insolvency, winding up, trusts, wills, probates and employment contract cases, and patent and copyright.
- Queen's Bench Division: handling everything else. This is by far the busiest division and therefore has the greatest number of judges, followed by the family and then chancery divisions.

The High Court usually sits in the same places as the Crown Court, and appeals go to the Court of Appeal Civil Division in London.

Court of Appeal

This is split into two parts:

- *Civil* headed by the Master of the Rolls and staffed by senior judges known as Lords Justice of Appeal.

- *Criminal* division is similarly staffed and headed by the Lord Chief Justice. Both courts have power to increase or decrease awards or sentences.

Self-assessment question 16.2

You work for a multinational company based in England, which has recently received some overseas trainees who need to gain an overview of English legal practice. Write a report to the trainees outlining what you believe to be the principal differences between civil law and criminal law.

Feedback on page 163

16.3 The role of European law in the English legal system

As a member of the European Union (EU) the UK is required to abide by EU laws and regulations. This is potentially a huge subject area and is well beyond our scope here, but we must focus on the aspect of EU law that most affects purchasing and supply. This is the subject of EU procurement directives. You should note that these apply only to certain types of organisation and certain levels of expenditure, the minimum levels of which are referred to as 'thresholds'.

Learning activity 16.3

By talking to colleagues or by, for example, accessing the CIPS website, research EU procurement directives and try to identify what kinds of organisation are subject to them and what the spending thresholds might be.

Feedback on page 164

The general principles of EU directives are aimed at achieving clarity and competition in public procurement whenever a contract is to be awarded whose value exceeds a certain threshold, by laying down a few rules generally regarded as being based on common sense.

The directives fall into two groups:

1   those governing the traditional areas of public procurement
2   those dealing with water, energy, transport and telecommunications.

The directives require that contracts over a certain threshold be advertised in the *Official Journal of the European Union* (OJEU). Advertisements adhere to a prescribed format and include details of the contracting authority, relevant standards and specifications, and the time limit for the submission of tenders, and the chosen award procedure must be performed 'online'.

16

There is a choice of three procedures: open, restricted or negotiated.

- The open procedure allows any supplier to bid: that is, all interested parties may submit a tender. Contracts are usually advertised using open procedures when the most important consideration in purchasing is price.
- The restricted procedure comprises a two-stage process whereby suppliers need to pre-qualify before being allowed to put their bid forward. This procedure is most often employed when there is a need to establish whether or not firms bidding possess the relevant skills or qualifications. This is the most commonly used procedure because it enables the bidding process to be restricted to suitably qualified providers.
- The negotiated procedure can be used only in limited circumstances such as where there is only one source of supply, where no suitable bids have been received in response to a previous notice using the open or restricted procedure, or in the event of emergency.

It is a legal requirement that award criteria be included in the tender document and are adhered to when subsequently awarding the contract. Thus, if price is given as the only award criterion, the contract *must* be awarded based on best price. For this reason, most purchasers that are subject to EU directives will give 'best value' as the main award criterion or will give a range of criteria.

Self-assessment question 16.3

Write an essay of no more than 250 words explaining the nature and role of EU directives and how they might affect purchasing in the UK.

Feedback on page 164

Revision question

Now try the revision question for this session on page 198.

Summary

In this study session we have begun to examine the law and its effect on purchasing and supply. You should now know that this area of law is a mixture of common law and statute and that actions (or 'suits') brought as a result of purchasing and supply disputes fall under the heading of civil law.

You should also have an understanding of the basic roles of:

- magistrates' courts
- county courts
- Crown Courts
- the High Court
- Court of Appeal.

You should also have a basic understanding of the role and nature of EU procurement directives.

Suggested further reading

The recommended texts for this unit do not really contain much information about legal issues because they are regarded as being highly specialised in nature. However, the CIPS website contains a wealth of useful information that you might like to access. If this topic interests you, you could obtain from your local public library a copy of Griffiths and Griffiths (2002).

Feedback on learning activities and self-assessment questions

Feedback on learning activity 16.1

The main statutes that you should have identified are:

- Sale of Goods Act 1979: this concerns several aspects of the quality of *goods* that are *sold* (note: it does not cover services or goods obtained by barter or exchange). The Sale and Supply of Goods Act 1994 amended this statute by altering the basic definition of what is acceptable quality.
- Supply of Goods and Services Act 1982: this extended the provisions of the above statute to cover services and supply by barter or exchange.
- Unfair Contract Terms Act 1977: its main provision is to prevent the insertion of clauses deemed 'unfair' into contracts.

Feedback on self-assessment question 16.1

You should have said that statutes originate from Parliament where laws or Acts of Parliament are voted on and brought into being ('enacted'). These affect a wide variety of subjects or aspects of life, although the ones we are concerned with affect contracts and other aspects of purchasing and supply.

Common law is law that has existed for many years, in some cases centuries. It is not written down but is assumed to be known by everyone.

You might have stated that decisions made in cases, usually known as 'case law' or 'judicial precedent', can affect future interpretation of both statutes and common law.

Feedback on learning activity 16.2

Feedback to this activity is contained in the subsequent text.

Feedback on self-assessment question 16.2

The principal differences are:

1   Civil law is designed to provide individuals with compensation; criminal law is designed to punish transgressors.

16

2 Civil law normally operates in different courts from the criminal law.
3 Civil cases need to be proven on the balance of probabilities, and a criminal one beyond reasonable doubt. Thus the 'burden of proof' is much greater in criminal cases.
4 A civil case is a suit, a criminal one a prosecution.
5 Civil suits are brought by private individuals, groups or corporations; prosecutions are normally brought by state organisations or agencies.

Feedback on learning activity 16.3

Briefly, the kinds of organisation that are subject to EU directives are:

- Public sector organisations such as local authorities, the National Health Service (NHS), the police and so on.
- Private sector organisations that provide public services or utilities in 'restricted' (that is: not subject to genuine competition) markets. Examples would include most of the public sector organisations that were privatised during the 1980s such as Powergen and other energy providers, as well as water companies such as Severn Trent.

You should note that 'ordinary' private sector organisations are *not* subject to EU directives, and that some recently privatised organisations such as BT are no longer subject to them because the markets in which they operate are regarded as being sufficiently competitive.

The expenditure thresholds change frequently but typically might be €150,000.

Feedback on self-assessment question 16.3

You should have identified that EU directives seek to bring an element of competition to public sector purchasing. They affect only expenditure that is likely to be above certain thresholds and only public sector organisations and private sector ones that provide public utilities or services.

It is difficult to gauge what effect they will have on UK purchasing, but they will probably have the effect of meaning that more and more public sector contracts will be awarded to non-UK suppliers, particularly with the recent increase of the EU to 25 countries.

Contract formation

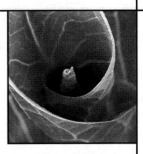

'A verbal contract isn't worth the paper it is written on.'
Samuel Goldwyn

Introduction

In this study session we start to look at how a contract is formed. Purchasers enter into contracts very frequently, and knowledge about how they are formed will stand you in good stead. You should remember that the definition of a contract that underpins all of this is 'a legally binding agreement between two or more parties': nothing more, nothing less. Do not worry about the 'or more'; it tends to confuse the issue. Just concentrate on the 'legally binding agreement between two parties'. How such an agreement comes into being is the subject of this study session.

Session learning objectives

After completing this session you should be able to:

17.1 Explain the nature and significance of 'offer' and 'acceptance' in contract formation.
17.2 Explain the nature and significance of 'consideration', 'intention to be legally bound' and 'capacity' in contract formation.
17.3 Describe templates and standard contractual forms.

Unit content coverage

Learning outcome

Identify the essential elements of a legally binding agreement.

Learning objective

4.2 Outline the key components of the formation of contract.
  • Offer
  • Acceptance
  • Consideration
  • Intention to be legally bound
  • Capacity

Prior knowledge

None, although study session 16 would 'set the scene' to some extent.

Resources

None, although consulting your legal representatives at work might be useful.

Timing

You should set aside about 2½ hours to read and complete this session, including learning activities, self-assessment questions, the suggested further reading (if any) and the revision question.

17.1 The nature and significance of 'offer' and 'acceptance' in contract formation

In this section we start looking at the basic elements required to form a contract, and will complete this in section 17.2 below. The thing you *must* remember is that a legally binding contract requires all of the elements mentioned in the unit content coverage (offer, acceptance, consideration, intention to create legal relations, capacity and agreement) to be in place. If, in any agreement, any of these elements is not in place, *no contract exists* even if both parties think that one does exist and intend that there should be one. In this section we shall focus on the elements of 'offer' and 'acceptance'.

Offer

This can be in the form of an offer to buy or an offer to sell. In 'simple' (that is, private) contracts this can be a person saying 'would you like to buy this widget for £5?', which would be an offer to sell, or 'I will give you £5 for that widget', which would be an offer to buy.

To be valid an offer must:

- be communicated, so that the other party may accept or reject it
- be definite in substance, and
- be distinguished from an 'invitation to treat' (see below).

Additionally, an offer may be communicated in writing, in words, or by conduct. There is no general requirement that an agreement must be in writing, and an offer may be made to a particular person, to a group of persons, or to the whole world.

Learning activity 17.1

We have talked about 'offers' in general terms, but which documents in commercial purchasing would normally be considered an 'offer'? Try to find out the answer to this by asking colleagues or your organisation's legal representatives.

Feedback on page 170

You should note that an enquiry (RFQ) sent by a buyer to a potential supplier is known as an **invitation to treat** and, as such, has no legal consequence whatsoever. The same principle applies to a telephone call to a potential supplier asking whether they sell a certain item, to suppliers' catalogues, to the display of goods on supermarket shelves or in a shop window, and to advertisements.

Acceptance

This is the person to whom the offer was made saying 'yes' (or words to that effect). Acceptance can also be *implied* – no words spoken or written, but the person's conduct implying acceptance. In terms of commercial purchasing, acceptance is usually one of the following:

- acknowledgement of the order
- a purchase order sent to a supplier in response to a quotation.

Note: if either of these documents differs *in any respect* from the original document it is responding to, it is not acceptance but a '**counter-offer**', which destroys the original offer and, for a legally binding contract to exist, must be accepted in turn. An acceptance is a final and unqualified assent to all the terms of the offer, and has the following prerequisites:

- It must be made while the offer is still in force.
- It must be made by the offeree.
- It must exactly match the terms of the offer.
- It may be written, oral, or implied by conduct.
- A person cannot accept an offer of which they have no knowledge.

As stated in the introduction to this study session, offer and acceptance, taken together, form an **agreement**, sometimes known as '**consensus *ad idem***', usually translated as 'an agreement on the same thing' or 'a meeting of the minds'. Essentially it means that both parties to the contract are in agreement as to the nature of the subject of the contract (that is, the product or service being bought and sold). This is easy when you are discussing the contract face to face with a seller with the subject of the contract at hand. It is less easy when you are buying by description over the telephone or from a catalogue, when 'offeror' and 'offeree' might have entirely different conceptions of the nature (for example size, robustness, material, etc) of the item.

For this reason it is usual to reserve the right to take a suitable time to inspect items bought by description to make sure that they are as you intended. Also, most catalogues have phrases such as 'money refunded if not absolutely delighted'. This saves a great deal of time and trouble with legal action in the event of a distant customer deciding that the item, upon receipt, does not bear much resemblance to the photograph or drawing in the catalogue.

There is no self-assessment question for this section. Instead, these topics are covered in self-assessment question 17.1 below.

17.2 The nature and significance of 'consideration', 'intention to be legally bound', 'capacity' and 'legality' in forming contracts

In this section we shall continue from where we left off in section 17.1 above and complete our examination of the elements that are required to be in place before a legally binding contract can be said to exist.

17

Consideration

This is what the buyer gives to the seller in exchange for the goods or services. It is usually money, although the law states only that consideration must be 'something of value', thus recognising barter, swapping and exchanging one service for another or the exchange of a service for goods, or vice versa. In most instances in commercial purchasing, however, 'consideration' is the payment. It does not matter whether this payment is made by cash, cheque or credit transfer.

Intention to be legally bound

This is often known as 'intention to create legal relations'.

Here, both parties must intend that there should be a legally binding contract. In commercial purchasing, what usually happens is that a buyer forwards a document labelled 'purchase order' to a supplier, with terms and conditions on the reverse. Then the supplier responds with a document labelled 'acknowledgement', possibly also with terms and conditions on the reverse. Any situation such as this will be deemed by a court as an intention by both parties to create legal relations. Most legal actions under this heading have arisen from 'domestic disputes'.

Capacity

Everyone over the age of 18 has capacity to contract for themselves unless they are drunk or under the influence of drugs or suffering mental disorder. In commercial purchasing we need to consider which staff members have capacity to contract on behalf of the company for which they work.

Learning activity 17.2

Try to find out, by talking to colleagues or your organisation's legal representatives, which staff members have capacity to contract on behalf of your organisation.

Feedback on page 171

Legality

The law will not support a contract for an illegal purpose even if all of the necessary 'elements' are in place. Obvious, really!

The following has no direct bearing on the *essential elements* of a contract, but you should note that a contract need not be in any particular form. There is no need for a document labelled 'contract' for a contract to be legally binding. The law recognises verbal contracts, although to win an action under a verbal contract you would need independent witness!

17

Self-assessment question 17.1

This question also covers topics from section 17.1 above and is in the form of a short case study.

You enter a shop and see a sign saying 'Mars bars 40p'. You say to the shopkeeper 'a Mars bar, please'. The shopkeeper places the Mars bar on the counter and asks for 40p. You pay the 40p, take the Mars bar and leave the shop.

Does a contract exist? Give reasons for your answer.

Feedback on page 171

17.3 Templates and standard contractual forms

We have already said that a contract does not need to be in any particular form (see section 17.2 above), but the number of clauses required in a contract can be significant, and individual clauses can become complex, as you will find out in study session 18. It can therefore take a long time to prepare and negotiate a contract. To reduce the amount of effort required, buyers and sellers can agree to use a standard form of contract. This can be a 'model form' of contract, which is prepared independently of the contracting parties by some external body, or an internally prepared standard contract.

Model forms of contract

These comprehensive documents attempt to give a fair balance of contractual responsibilities and liabilities to both buyer and seller. Bodies such as the Chartered Institute of Purchasing and Supply, the Institution of Civil Engineers and various trade associations publish model forms of contract. Members can access the CIPS one through the CIPS website.

The model forms appropriate for a particular industry will be widely known and generally accepted within the industry. For example, the model forms published by the Institution of Civil Engineers will be well understood within the construction industry. Most suppliers will accept the standard forms, thus saving considerable cost and time in negotiating a complex construction contract.

Company standard contracts

Alternatively, where a company has recurring requirements for a product or service, standard contracts developed in-house can be used. Once suppliers accept a standard contract, there will not need to be any further time spent on negotiating contracts.

17

Learning activity 17.3

Has your organisation any standard contracts for the purchase of goods or services? If you are not sure, try asking colleagues to find out. Assuming your organisation does have standard contracts, what do they cover?

Feedback on page 171

Now try this:

Self-assessment question 17.2

1   Why might you use a model form of contract?
2   Note down any problems you might envisage from using model contract forms.

Feedback on page 172

Revision question

Now try the revision question for this session on page 198.

Summary

In this study session we have considered the essential elements of a contract, and you should now be aware that any agreement that does *not* have:

* offer
* acceptance
* consideration
* capacity
* intention to create legal relations
* agreement

is *not* a legally binding contract.

We have also examined the role of model contract forms.

Feedback on learning activities and self-assessment questions

Feedback on learning activity 17.1

In commercial purchasing an offer is usually one of the following documents:

* a **purchase order** (an offer to buy when sent to a supplier without a preceding enquiry or quotation)

17

- a **quotation**, **bid** or **tender** from a supplier (an offer to sell).

Feedback on learning activity 17.2

The answer to this question is, in some people's view, deeply unsatisfactory, and is certainly prone to the criticism of being 'woolly'.

It is this: the only people with **absolute** capacity are the owner, partners, or board of directors. The position of capacity of employees is more difficult, and is as follows.

If the other party 'reasonably supposed' that you have capacity to contract on behalf of your company, you do in fact have that capacity. In practice, this supposition – 'reasonable' or otherwise – depends upon the individual's job title and/or job description, so that:

- People with job titles such as 'buyer', 'purchasing manager' etc clearly will be 'reasonably supposed' to have capacity to contract on behalf of their employers, as would 'sales managers' and so on.
- Equally clearly, people with job titles such as 'filing clerk', 'lavatory cleaner' etc will not.
- Problems arise with people whose job title is 'production manager', 'chief accountant' and so on. The apparent seniority of such job titles would lead many people to 'reasonably suppose' that those individuals have capacity to contract on behalf of their employers.
- The principle described above is known as 'apparent or ostensible authority'.

Feedback on self-assessment question 17.1

Your conclusion should be that a contract exists. The reasons are as follows:

The sign saying 'Mars bar 40p' is an invitation to treat. The contractual 'elements' are as follows:

- Offer: your requesting a Mars bar.
- Acceptance: the shopkeeper's placing it on the counter and asking for 40p.
- Consideration: 40p paid.
- Agreement: both parties know that the contract's subject is a Mars bar.
- Capacity: we assume that you and the shopkeeper are both over 18 and that the shopkeeper is the owner of the business. (Obviously you don't need to be over 18 to buy a Mars bar, but you do need to be over 18 to enter into a contract. If the shopkeeper were a school girl or boy doing a Saturday job they would *not* have capacity to enter into a contract.)
- Intention: not really relevant, but you clearly intended to buy the Mars bar and the shopkeeper intended to sell it.

Feedback on learning activity 17.3

Specific feedback is difficult, but organisations typically have standard contracts for the purchase of either goods or services. Sometimes these are

17

combined within the same standard contract. Larger organisations may have more specialised contracts dealing with particular products or services depending on what key products or services they purchase.

Feedback on self-assessment question 17.2

1   Appropriate model forms – that is, ones widely used in a particular industry – will be generally accepted by suppliers and therefore avoid potentially costly and lengthy contractual negotiations.
2   Although model forms might purport to be fair to both parties, they should be checked to ensure that they adequately cover the purchaser's position.

17

Study session 18
Contract terms and conditions

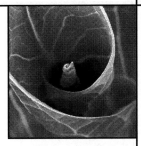

Why does the 'small print' make everything more complicated?

Introduction

In this study session we shall consider terms and conditions of contract. This is the 'small print' that accompanies every purchase order and probably every other commercial document. Terms and conditions play a very important part in contract formation, and we shall examine this in some detail.

Session learning objectives

After completing this session you should be able to:

18.1 Explain the role of terms and conditions in contracts.
18.2 Distinguish between 'conditions' and 'warranties' and between 'express' and 'implied' terms of a contract.
18.3 Explain the meaning of special contract terms such as force majeure, retention of title, transfer of risk, payment, etc.

Unit content coverage

Learning outcome

Identify the essential elements of a legally binding agreement

Learning objective

4.3 Explain the concept of contract terms and conditions – expressed and implied:
  • Defining terms and conditions
  • Understanding the need for terms
  • Examining basic terms: termination, payment, ownership, risk.

Prior knowledge

Study session 17.

Resources

None specific but a knowledge of your organisation's contract terms would be useful.

18

Timing

You should set aside about 3 hours to read and complete this session, including learning activities, self-assessment questions, the suggested further reading (if any) and the revision question.

18.1 The role of terms and conditions of contract

This section includes the nature of 'small print': why it exists, and the 'battle of the forms'.

What are terms and conditions?

In law the word used should be 'term'. In practice, however, the words 'term' and 'condition' have different meanings. As we shall see, a term can be either a 'condition' or a 'warranty'.

So what exactly is a term?

Essentially, terms form the details of a contract and can be seen as a statement by either party as being the 'rules' by which they intend the 'game' of contracting to be played. The fact that they are often relegated to the reverse of the order or quotation (if they appear at all) and are frequently printed in a type size so small as to be barely legible causes many people to regard them as being irrelevant. This view, however, is mistaken. The fact is that the terms are part of an offer or counter-offer (see study session 17) and can have the effect of rendering what was intended to be 'acceptance' a 'counter-offer'. This is because the buyer's terms will be worded in a way that protects the buyer's interests, the seller's terms will usually protect the seller's interests, and in practice there will usually be a conflict between the two sets of terms and conditions.

These make up the 'small print' on the reverse of many companies' purchase orders. In practice, they are ignored by many buyers. Potentially, however, they are important, and we shall examine the nature of this importance. Remember, buyers have terms and conditions of purchase; sellers have terms and conditions of sale.

Learning activity 18.1

Try to find your organisation's terms and conditions. They should be on the reverse of your purchase orders. If not, ask a colleague about them and then identify three specific terms and note down what they mean. If your organisation does not have any formal terms, note down what you think might be the possible consequences of this.

Feedback on page 179

The 'battle of the forms'

This situation arises from the documents (or 'forms') that can sometimes go back and forth between buyer and seller. It concerns the fact that, if the various forms (quotation, order, acknowledgement, etc) differ from each other in some way, usually because of conflicts in the terms, they will constitute *counter-offers* (see study session 17) rather than *acceptance*. This would mean that formal acceptance of the original offer never takes place and no contract exists. For example, a quotation ('offer') is received from a supplier and a purchase order is sent to the supplier, but while the main part is in agreement with the quotation the terms differ, and so the order constitutes a 'counter-offer'. The supplier then acknowledges the order on a document containing its own terms, and this is another 'counter-offer'. Remember that any 'counter-offer' has to be accepted for a legally binding contract to exist.

The rule is as follows. If no query has arisen during the performance of the contract and the seller delivers the goods to the buyer, if the buyer accepts them, a legally binding contract is deemed to have come into existence, with the prevailing terms being contained in the *last document* that passed between the parties. This is sometimes known as 'the last document rule', and buyers should be very careful of it because, often, the last document is likely to be either the seller's acknowledgement or advice note, both of which will probably contain the seller's terms.

You should note that this rule applies only where there has been no previous formal 'acceptance'.

You can try to ensure that the battle of the forms does not arise and that contracts are awarded subject to your terms by:

*   sending enquiries with your terms and stipulating that sellers *must* respond by completing and returning a copy of the enquiry document
*   sending acknowledgement copies of each purchase order, which the supplier is supposed to sign and return
*   negotiating and agreeing the contract with the supplier, including terms and conditions.

Self-assessment question 18.1

A difficult one! Try to draw a diagram to illustrate a typical 'battle of the forms' by indicating the documents that might pass between buyer and seller and their legal role. The first one is given to you.

Figure 18.1

Buyer	Invitation to treat (no legal significance)	Seller

Feedback on page 180

18.2 Conditions, warranties and express or implied terms

Conditions and warranties

As we said in the previous section, 'terms' can be divided into 'conditions' and 'warranties'. Here we shall examine the differences between each.

Earlier we made the point that, legally speaking, we should use the word 'term' rather than 'condition' as both have a slightly different meaning. A **term** can be either:

- a **condition**: these are terms that are crucial to the performance of the contract, or
- a **warranty** (not to be confused with a type of guarantee). These are terms of lesser importance to the performance of the contract.

This distinction is important because of the difference in remedies (solutions or settlements) in the event of a breach.

If a supplier breaches a condition the buyer may take one of the following courses of action:

- rescind the contract (return both parties to where they were before the contract was made)
- repudiate the contract and avoid the outstanding obligations (duties of the contract)
- seek an order from the court for 'specific performance' (force the supplier to perform their contractual obligations)
- receive damages (set by the court as compensation for the breach).

If a supplier breaches a warranty the buyer can only sue for damages, and the court would only award these so as to compensate for losses directly associated with the breach.

Whether or not a term is a condition or a warranty would be decided by the court in the event of litigation.

Learning activity 18.2

Take the terms that you identified in learning activity 18.1 above and try to identify which you think would be considered 'conditions' and which would be 'warranties'. Note down your answers.

Feedback on page 181

'Express' or 'implied' terms

- **Express** terms are clearly stated and agreed between the parties. Examples might be price, delivery date and so on.
- **Implied** terms are not always mentioned but are assumed to exist and can form part of the contract. This might appear to be a difficult notion but an example would be the right of the seller to sell the goods, which would be assumed (by both parties) to exist without being discussed.

18

Some implied terms derive from legislation so that, for example, section 14 of the Sale of Goods Act 1979 states that it is implied in all contracts for the sale of goods that they shall be fit for the purpose for which they are sold.

Self-assessment question 18.2

Write a memorandum of not more than 200 words on the differences between conditions and warranties and between express and implied terms. Use examples to illustrate the points you make.

Feedback on page 181

18.3 'Special' contract terms

Potentially there are many of these, and different ones might be applied to different contracts. Typical 'special' terms might include *'force majeure'*, retention of title, liquidated damages and transfer of risk.

'Force majeure'

This relates to circumstances outside the control of either party to a contract that might prevent them from carrying out their contractual duties. It is usually sellers that include such contracts, and they might include such a clause to absolve them of responsibility for late delivery or non-delivery due to (for example) transport strikes, bad weather, civil commotion and so on. You are most likely to see such clauses on contracts for goods being imported, because the risk of loss of goods or delay is much greater when the journey is long, complex and with many different stages.

Retention of title/passing of property

This refers to when your organisation believes that the item should become its property. Typically, this would be when the goods have been physically accepted and have been certified as being satisfactory. Many suppliers, however, will insist that property passes only when the goods have been paid for in full. This is likely to be a rather different time from 'satisfactory delivery'.

Learning activity 18.3

Try to find out, by asking colleagues, if necessary, whether your organisation uses a contract clause to stipulate when property passes from suppliers. If it does have such a clause, how does it work? Note down your answer.

Feedback on page 181

18

Liquidated damages

Clauses relating to this are often inserted into large contracts and seek to protect the buyer against late or unsatisfactory completion of the contract. They should relate to damages *directly* related to the poor contract performance by the seller. Typical wording might be:

'In the event of delay in completing this contract, the seller shall forfeit 1% of the contract price for each week of delay up to a maximum of six weeks.'

These clauses are usually enforceable without recourse to court, provided both parties have accepted them as a clause of the contract. The buyer would usually do this by simply deducting the stated amount from the payment. However, if the seller were to challenge such a clause in court as claiming excessive recompense, tests for the validity of the clause would be:

* Are the liquidated damages a genuine pre-estimate of losses?
* Is the level of damages excessive and unacceptable given the maximum actual damage foreseeable?

If the answer to either of these questions is 'yes', the liquidated damages clause would be deemed a 'penalty' and would be unenforceable.

Passage of risk

'Risk' usually passes at the same time as property/title. This is important, because when risk passes from seller to buyer, the buyer must undertake insurance on the items as necessary. This is particularly important for goods being imported, and there are several possibilities as to where in the journey risk passes. These could include:

* the seller's gate
* arrival of the goods at the dock in the port of exit in the seller's country
* arrival of the goods at the port of entry in the buyer's country
* arrival of the goods at the buyer's premises.

There are other possibilities, and it is important for buyer and seller to agree so that the buyer can undertake to insure the goods for the remainder of their journey.

This is by no means an exhaustive list of possible 'special' terms, but these are the aspects of a contract most frequently covered by such terms.

Self-assessment question 18.3

Scroggins Machinery Supplies Ltd contracted to sell a piece of machinery to AGZ Ltd. The contract was subject to a clause stating that property in the machine would not pass until AGZ had paid for it in full. The machine was destroyed in a fire at AGZ's premises before it had been paid for. Who should bear the risk in this situation?

Feedback on page 181

Revision question

Now try the revision question for this session on page 198.

Summary

In this study session we have examined various aspects of terms and conditions of contract, or *terms*, as they are more correctly known. You should now be aware of:

- the basic role of terms and their importance in contracts
- the differences between conditions and warranties and how each might affect a contract
- the meaning and nature of some special terms of contract.

You should note that this study session only 'scratches the surface' of what is a very complex subject and one that you will study in more depth later in your CIPS studies.

Feedback on learning activities and self-assessment questions

Feedback on learning activity 18.1

Specific feedback is impossible but typical purchaser's terms might include the following:

- **Definitions**
  - The full name of your company as well as that of the seller.
  - A full description of the item.
- **Acknowledgement**: a stipulation that your purchase order should be acknowledged in writing.
- **Variations**: a stipulation that no variations to the contract are acceptable without your written agreement.
- **Inspection/testing**: a term that sets out to allow your company adequate time to perform a thorough inspection of incoming goods, where considered necessary. Typically, this would be a minimum of three days.
- **Delivery/packing**: a stipulation that this should be in accordance with the instructions contained in the purchase order.
- **Passing of property**: an indication of when your company believes that the item should become the buyer's property. Typically, this would be when the goods have been physically accepted and have been certified as being satisfactory.
- **Time**: it is usual to include a clause stating that 'Time shall be of the essence of the order'. Without such a clause it is virtually impossible to take legal action against a supplier for late delivery.
- **Damage/loss in transit**: it is usual to include a clause that states that the seller should be liable for any such damage or loss.
- **Payment**: the buyer should include a clause stating the terms of payment preferred by the buyer's organisation.
- **Assignment/subcontracting**: it is usual to state that no part of the contract shall be given to a third party without the buyer's written consent.
- **Rejection**: it is usual to insert a clause to establish rules for the possible rejection of goods supplied.

18

If your organisation does not have terms it is likely that all its contracts will be subject to suppliers' terms, which will almost certainly be contrary to its interests.

Feedback on self-assessment question 18.1

Your diagram might look something like figure 18.2:

Figure 18.2

Buyer
Seller
Invitation to treat (no legal significance)
Quotation (seller's terms)
Offer
Purchase order (buyer's terms)
Counter-offer
Acknowledgement (seller's terms)
Counter-offer
Packing note (seller's terms) (no legal significance)

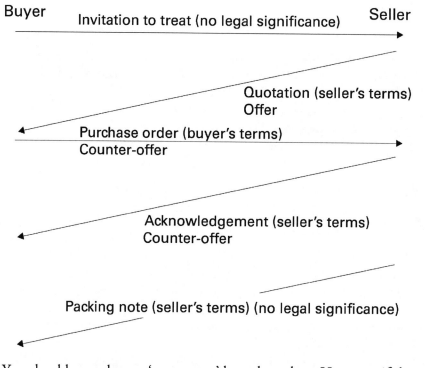

You should note that no 'acceptance' has taken place. However, if there is no query or problem the goods will be delivered and, if acceptable, will be accepted. There is a legally binding contract because the conduct of *both* parties (delivery and acceptance) would lead one to *presume* that there was one.

The terms binding on the contract are contained on the *last document* to pass between the parties. (In the illustration these are the seller's terms.)

An alternative view might look like figure 18.3:

Figure 18.3

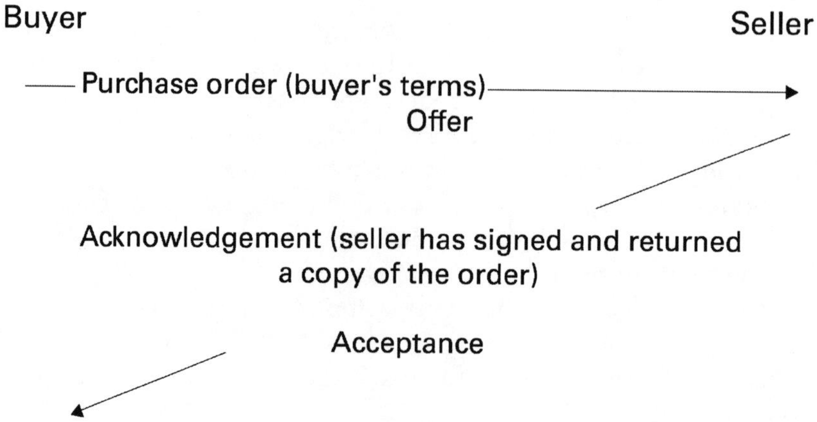

Buyer
Seller
Purchase order (buyer's terms)
Offer
Acknowledgement (seller has signed and returned a copy of the order)
Acceptance

Feedback on learning activity 18.2

Again, specific feedback is impossible but, typically, conditions would be terms relating to such 'core' aspects of a contract as price, delivery, acceptance or rejection of goods. Warranties might be terms relating to such issues as insurance during transit, packaging and labelling, all of which might be regarded as being more peripheral to the contract.

Feedback on self-assessment question 18.2

Your answer should state clearly that conditions are terms that go to the heart of the contract and whose performance is crucial to the contract, whereas warranties are more minor terms. You should state that the remedies for breach of a contract are much stronger than those for a breach of a warranty and may include repudiation, rescission and specific performance as well as damages. Remedies for a breach of warranty are limited to damages.

An express term is stated clearly in the contract, whereas an implied term is understood by both parties to exist without specific reference to it, such as the right of the seller to sell the goods.

Feedback on learning activity 18.3

Specific feedback is impossible owing to the nature of the activity. If your organisation does have such a clause it could be:

- that title/property passes when the goods are paid for in full
- that it passes upon delivery and acceptance.

You should note that some suppliers would have a clause in their terms of sale that it passes upon delivery, meaning that, as soon as the goods are unloaded from the transport at your goods inward, they are yours. This is not an advisable state of affairs to be in from a purchaser's viewpoint, because the supplier could claim payment even if the goods were not satisfactory.

Feedback on self-assessment question 18.3

Your answer should state that the machine was sold subject to a retention of title clause and so the risk is Scroggins'.

Privity of contract

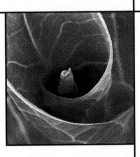

Introduction

Privity of contract is an important principle that can have a major effect on contract formation. Basically, it means that only the two parties that entered into a contractual agreement can be bound by it. This sounds entirely logical (and is!), but there are a few exceptions, as we shall see further into the study session.

Session learning objectives

After completing this session you should be able to:

19.1 Explain the concept of privity of contract and its effect on contract formation and operation.
19.2 Give examples of exceptions to the 'privity' concept and state reasons for their existence.
19.3 Describe the main provisions of the Contracts (Rights of Third Parties) Act 1999.

Unit content coverage

Learning outcome

Identify the essential elements of a legally binding agreement

Learning objective

4.4 Explain privity and exceptions to the doctrine of privity: including Contracts (Rights of Third Parties) Act 1999:
  • Understanding when legal liability moves from the buyer to another party

Prior knowledge

Study sessions 17 and 18.

Resources

Access to the internet.

Timing

You should set aside about 2 hours to read and complete this session, including learning activities, self-assessment questions, the suggested further reading (if any) and the revision question.

19.1 The concept of privity of contract and its effect on contract formation

There is a principle inherent in common law that only a party to the contract may sue or be sued upon it. In other words, only the buyer and seller in any contractual agreement can take any legal action based on the contract. No other person has any rights or obligations whatsoever as far as the contract is concerned. This principle is known as 'privity of contract'.

Learning activity 19.1

A problem with privity of contract is that a *subcontractor* is usually unable to sue or be sued by the purchaser because of this principle. Try to find out, by talking to colleagues or your company's legal representatives, how a purchaser might seek to hold a subcontractor liable for a breach of contract where the only direct contract the purchaser has is with the main contractor.

Feedback on page 187

Recently, opinion has change somewhat on this principle of privity and exceptions to the principle will be covered in the next section.

Now try this.

Self-assessment question 19.1

A manufacturing company wished to ensure that the price of its product sold to consumers would be artificially high. To do this they had contracts with wholesalers that stipulated that wholesalers would buy from them at a fixed price and that the wholesalers would, in turn, insist that retailers would sell to consumers at a fixed minimum price. To do this they inserted two clauses into the contracts with wholesalers:

(a) If you sell as a retailer, you will sell to a customer at no less than £50 per unit.

(b) If you sell other than as a retailer, you must pass on clause (a) in your contract.

One wholesaler complied exactly with this, but a retailer to whom they sold the products sold them to consumers at less than the stipulated price, in

19

(continued on next page)

Self-assessment question 19.1 *(continued)*

clear breach of clause (a). The manufacturer sued the retailer but lost. Try to work out why this might be. (This is based on a real case.)

Feedback on page 187

19.2 Exceptions to the 'privity' concept

In section 19.1 above we looked at the 'privity' concept, but you should note that there are exceptions to it. First, there is the matter of 'collateral contracts'. This is when a supplier, such as a car dealer, provides for the end user a product bearing the manufacturer's guarantee or warranty. You do not need to learn legal cases, but the 'collateral' principle is demonstrated very well by the case of *Shanklin Pier* v *Detel Products Ltd* [1951].

Here, a purchaser placed a contract for the painting of a pier with a contractor and stipulated that a certain brand of paint be used because the paint supplier had said that it would last seven years. In the event, it lasted only three months, and it was held that the purchaser had a direct claim against the paint manufacturer *collaterally* to any claim that the contractor might have.

Learning activity 19.2

Reflect on reading about privity and collateral contracts and try to identify any contracts that have been placed in your workplace that might be subject to the 'collateral' principle.

Feedback on page 187

A second type of exception to the 'privity' concept concerns the Contracts (Rights of Third Parties) Act 1999. We shall look at this in section 19.3 below and cover both sections in self-assessment question 19.2 below. There is therefore no separate self-assessment question for section 19.2 above.

19.3 The Contracts (Rights of Third Parties) Act 1999

Another exception to the 'privity' concept is this Act of Parliament, which came into effect on 11 May 2000. This lays down the principle that a third party may enforce rights under a contract where:

- The third party is expressly given the right to do so under the contract.
- The contract purports to confer a benefit on the third party.
- The parties to the contract have not made it clear that they intended to exclude the third party from having the right to enforce it.

There is more detail in the Act, as you would expect, that is beyond our scope here, but much of it relates to such issues as:

- Identification of the third parties. Typically these might be agents or subcontractors.

19

- The concept of positive and negative benefit. The idea of 'negative benefit' might seem strange, but essentially it concerns such issues as an undertaking to *not* do something.
- The court having limited authority to reduce third-party rights and the fact that third-party rights cannot be rescinded (cancelled) or varied without their consent.

Learning activity 19.3

Try to find out more about the Act, including examples of its use, from the internet. This will almost certainly involve using a 'search engine'.

Feedback on page 187

The Act does not apply to:

- bills of exchange, promissory notes and other negotiable instruments (such things as cheques)
- company memoranda or articles of association (these are the legal rules that govern how a company is established)
- contracts of employment
- some contracts for the carriage of goods.

Self-assessment question 19.2

Write a report (of no more than 200 words) to subordinates or colleagues indicating the exceptions to the 'privity' concept that relates to contracts. Provide details of the kinds of situation that such exceptions relate to.

Feedback on page 187

Revision question

Now try the revision question for this session on page 198.

Summary

In this study session we have examined the concept of 'privity' of contract: the basic rule that only the two parties that make the contractual agreement have any rights or liabilities under it. We have also considered exceptions to that legal principle, namely:

- collateral contracts
- Contracts (Rights of Third Parties) Act 1999.

Suggested further reading

If this topic interests you, you could obtain from your local public library a copy of Griffiths and Griffiths (2002).

Feedback on learning activities and self-assessment questions

Feedback on learning activity 19.1

This is a difficult one. Privity of contract will prevent the purchaser from suing the subcontractor directly, and so the best way to resolve the problem is to ensure that the main contractor is contractually liable for all the actions and omissions of the subcontractor. The main contractor can always sue the subcontractor to recover losses paid out to the purchaser.

Feedback on self-assessment question 19.1

The manufacturer lost because they only had a contract with the wholesaler, and therefore could not sue the retailer. Only the wholesaler could successfully sue the retailer. However, the manufacturer could not sue the wholesaler because the wholesaler had not broken the contract with the manufacturer, and in fact had done all that they were obliged to do. The wholesaler *could* sue the retailer but would get nothing because they had not suffered any loss.

The real case referred to is *Dunlop* v *Selfridge* [1915]. You might like to check it out if you read Griffiths and Griffiths (2002), which is cited in the suggested further reading at the end of the session.

Feedback on learning activity 19.2

Specific feedback is impossible, but typical contracts that may be subject to the collateral principle might be hire-purchase contracts, where the purchaser would have rights against both the supplier of the item and the finance company that would be the actual owner of it. Similarly, if your company has insured a piece of equipment with a group of Lloyds underwriters acting in a syndicate, it would have rights against each individual member of the syndicate.

Feedback on learning activity 19.3

There are several websites that will give more information about the Act and examples of its use, but there is no specific feedback as such.

Feedback on self-assessment question 19.2

Your answer should focus on collateral contract and the Contracts (Rights of Third Parties) Act 1999. You should say that collateral contracts typically relate to contracts with a supplier of products that, by implication, involve the original manufacturer of the product.

The Act confers rights on third parties, which are detailed in the text of this section.

19

Contract dispute resolution

'Talking is over-rated as a means of settling disputes.'
Tom Cruise

Introduction

No matter how carefully you draft contracts, or how good your relationship with suppliers, it is inevitable that disputes will occur from time to time. In this study session we shall look at the means available to settle such disputes. The first of these is negotiation, and it is likely that a very great percentage of disputes will be settled in this way. Then, in order of cost and difficulty, come adjudication and arbitration. Recourse to law (litigation) is very much the last resort, mainly because of its cost and the length of time it can take. There is also the fact that legal cases are in the public domain and may lead to bad publicity for the companies concerned.

Session learning objectives

After completing this session you should be able to:

20.1 Explain the role and significance of negotiation as a means of dispute resolution.
20.2 Explain the role and significance of adjudication and arbitration as means of dispute resolution.
20.3 Explain the role and significance of litigation as a means of dispute resolution.

Unit content coverage

This study session covers the following topics from the official CIPS unit content document:

Learning outcome

Identify the essential elements of a legally binding agreement

Learning objective

4.5 Describe different approaches to resolving contractual disputes.
  • Negotiation
  • Arbitration
  • Adjudication
  • Through a court of law

Prior knowledge

Study session 16.

Resources

None specific but a working knowledge of the preferred method(s) of dispute resolution in your workplace would be useful.

Timing

You should set aside about 2¾ hours to read and complete this session, including learning activities, self-assessment questions, the suggested further reading (if any) and the revision question.

20.1 The role and significance of negotiation as a means of dispute resolution

It is easy and tempting to suppose that every time you disagree with a supplier you take them to court. The fact is, however, that this action ('litigation') is usually the last resort.

Most claims and disputes can be settled by amicable negotiation leading to an agreement. This is the quickest and least costly method of settling disputes and, as every buyer should know, is the preferred first course of action should a dispute arise with a supplier. It *can* also have the effect of enhancing the relationship between buyer and seller.

You will study negotiation techniques elsewhere in your CIPS studies.

Learning activity 20.1

Think about a dispute with a supplier that might have happened where you work. If you do not have personal experience of such an occurrence, talk to colleagues. Was negotiation used as a first 'port of call' to resolve it? If so, did it work? Was your organisation's legal position considered first?

Feedback on page 193

Negotiation does have drawbacks:

- Agreement is not always reached, meaning that a more formal means of dispute resolution is needed.
- It is difficult to use for disputes with overseas suppliers.

Self-assessment question 20.1

Write a brief report (about 100 words) on how useful negotiation is as a form of dispute resolution.

Feedback on page 193

20.2 The role and significance of adjudication and arbitration as means of dispute resolution

Adjudication

This is a process of expert determination. The expert is appointed by agreement between the parties, either generally or to decide a particular issue. Provided the expert keeps within the terms of the appointment and shows no bias, there is no restriction on the way a decision can be reached. Generally, an adjudicator will focus on the facts of the dispute rather than on points of law, and you could think of adjudication as 'negotiation with a referee present'.

Adjudication is less formal, and generally quicker and less costly than arbitration and litigation. If the contract provides for the expert determination to be final and binding, a court will not interfere with the decision reached.

Learning activity 20.2

Reflect on your reading of adjudication and try to think of some disputes you have encountered at work that could have been resolved by adjudication.

Feedback on page 193

Arbitration

Arbitration is more formal than adjudication, and resembles litigation, although will generally be less costly. It is a semi-judicial process, with evidence being heard. Unlike the adjudicator, an arbitrator cannot be sued for negligence. If the parties to a contract are unable to settle a dispute by arbitration, then there is no alternative but to enter into litigation.

An arbitrator can be an individual, or an organisation such as the Advisory, Conciliation and Arbitration Service (ACAS), and is often agreed upon and included in the contract from the outset although both parties may appoint an arbitrator after a dispute has arisen. If a dispute has gone to court the judge may decide to refer it to arbitration.

Increasingly, arbitration is used to resolve disputes in international contracts owing to difficulties of bringing such disputes to court, and may include points of law as well as points of fact.

Self-assessment question 20.2

1   Which of the following best describes arbitration as a means of settling disputes?
(a) Adversarial action under procedural rules established under a country's constitution whose decisions are legally binding.

(continued on next page)

20

Self-assessment question 20.2 (continued)

(b) A process of expert determination where the expert is appointed by both parties.

(c) A process of expert determination where the expert is agreed between the parties at the outset and their details inserted in the contract.

(d) A process whereby both parties meet to discuss the dispute with a view to resolution.

2 Write down the main differences between adjudication and arbitration.

Feedback on page 193

20.3 The role and significance of litigation as a means of dispute resolution

Litigation is the term used to describe dispute resolution in the courts. It may be described as 'an adversarial action under procedural rules established under a country's constitution, which will provide a *legally binding* result'. Cases between businesses are usually heard in the High Court, often by a single judge, although the normal appeal process applies for a party not satisfied with the decision: through the Court of Appeal and, finally, the House of Lords.

Learning activity 20.3

Reflect on your reading of the text and compare it with what happens in your workplace. Working with colleagues, especially the organisation's legal representative, try to identify circumstances in which the organisation would seek legal remedy.

Feedback on page 194

Litigation tends to be complex, time-consuming and expensive, although under English law the successful party usually has costs reimbursed. Unfortunately, litigation would almost certainly ruin any relationship that had previously existed between a buyer and a supplier.

Self-assessment question 20.3

Draft a report of not more than 200 words to subordinates or colleagues outlining why you think that litigation should be used to resolve disputes only as a last resort.

Feedback on page 194

Revision question

Now try the revision question for this session on page 198.

20

Summary

In this study session we have examined methods of resolving disputes between buyer and seller. These are:

- Negotiation: the easiest and least costly method and the usual first 'port of call'.
- Adjudication: having an expert to assist the process.
- Arbitration: more formal, having an expert to decide on points of law, perhaps.
- Litigation: the last resort, being costly and time-consuming.

Feedback on learning activities and self-assessment questions

Feedback on learning activity 20.1

Specific feedback is impossible, but it is likely that negotiation would have been used before any other method of resolution was considered. Remember that when we say 'dispute', we do not necessarily mean a situation where there has been a real 'blood and thunder' argument. Disputes can start as 'problems' such as buyer and supplier having different interpretations of a contract term. Problems can turn into full-blown disputes, however, if not resolved quickly, and negotiation is the usual first course of action.

If you consider your legal position before entering into negotiation you can negotiate from a position of strength.

Feedback on self-assessment question 20.1

Negotiation is the easiest and cheapest method because no formal procedures or references to third parties are required. However, to succeed, willingness by both parties to reach a solution is required, and the main drawback is that resolution might not be arrived at. Also, it is difficult to negotiate with distant, especially overseas, suppliers owing to the logistics of arranging meetings. You could note that, increasingly, video conferencing is being used to overcome this last problem.

Feedback on learning activity 20.2

Specific feedback is impossible, but typically, if you are not satisfied with a supplier's performance and after negotiation/discussion you cannot reach agreement, you and the supplier might agree to go to adjudication. The type of dispute will probably be relatively minor where the sums of money at stake are not great.

Feedback on self-assessment question 20.2

1   The correct answer is (c).
2   The following are some of the differences between the two:
  - Adjudication is less formal than arbitration and is concerned more with the facts of the dispute than with points of law.

20

- An arbitrator is more likely to be agreed upon and stated in the contract at the outset than is an adjudicator.
- Arbitration is often used for international disputes.
- Adjudication is likely to be less costly and less time-consuming than arbitration.

Feedback on learning activity 20.3

Specific feedback is impossible because of the nature of the activity, but it is likely that your organisation would consider litigation only in extreme circumstances. This could be where a supplier had breached a contract in a fairly major way (as opposed to a minor breach that can be rectified quite easily). It might also arise in situations where your organisation had tried to resolve a dispute in some more amicable way, such as negotiation, but the supplier was not interested in any kind of discussion.

Remember also that, although we talk all the time about taking suppliers to court or resolving disputes that are caused by the supplier's actions, suppliers might take us to court. This might be, for example, because we had refused to accept delivery of goods that we had ordered or refused to pay for them, in either case perhaps because we no longer wanted them!

Feedback on self-assessment question 20.3

Your answer should contain the following points:

- It is very expensive and time-consuming.
- It will tend to destroy relationships that might have been built up over a long period of time.
- It might be difficult to continue your normal business activities while you wait for the action to come to court.
- It is very difficult to arrange in international contractual disputes.

Revision questions

Revision question for study session 1

Describe the main objectives and considerations of purchasing in:

1 Manufacturing companies.
2 Service providers.
3 Not-for-profit organisations.

Feedback on page 201

Revision question for study session 2

Explain the differences between quality control and quality assurance and discuss the ways in which buyers and suppliers may contribute to both processes.

Feedback on page 201

Revision question for study session 3

1 Explain the concept of economic order quantity (EOQ) indicating what it seeks to achieve and what its drawbacks might be.
2 Explain how the fixed order point method of re-ordering works.

Feedback on page 202

Revision question for study session 4

You are responsible for buying several items from international suppliers.

1 Explain in detail how you would decide what type of transport to use.
2 Indicate some of the hazards that packaging might have to withstand during international journeys.

Feedback on page 202

Revision question for study session 5

1 Explain why on-time delivery is important to a purchaser.
2 Describe the meaning of true, or total, lead time and identify the stages in this concept.
3 Explain why expediting and measuring suppliers' delivery performance are important and describe how you would carry these out.

Feedback on page 202

Revision question for study session 6

1. Explain the meaning of total acquisition cost including the factors that usually contribute to it.
2. Draw a diagram to illustrate how a supplier's price would be made up.
3. Identify and briefly describe five pricing policies.

Feedback on page 203

Revision question for study session 7

1. Define the meaning of a specification.
2. State and briefly explain two aspects of specifications that might have legal implications.
3. What contribution can buyers make to the preparation of a specification?
4. Explain the concept of tolerances.
5. State four requirements of a specification.

Feedback on page 203

Revision question for study session 8

Describe in detail five types of specification and the situations where each might be used.

Feedback on page 204

Revision question for study session 9

1. Give a brief explanation of some problems associated with the use of early supplier involvement (ESI).
2. List and briefly explain four problems commonly associated with specifications being written exclusively by technical staff.
3. Give a brief explanation of four reasons why buyers should know about specifications.
4. State five contributions that suppliers could make as part of the ESI process.
5. Identify two contributions that buyers could make during early buyer involvement when specifications have international aspects.

Feedback on page 204

Revision question for study session 10

1. Define the meaning and purpose of a budget.
2. Identify and briefly explain five characteristics of service quality.
3. Identify and briefly explain five characteristics of product quality.
4. Briefly explain the differences between 'special' and 'standard' items.

Feedback on page 205

Revision question for study session 11

Consider the following situations. Do you consider these to be ethical ways of dealing with suppliers? Explain the reasons for your answers.

1　In a competitive tendering exercise, your manager has informed you that a contract should be placed with one of the suppliers bidding. You later find out that the chief executive of the supplier organisation happens to be related to your manager. Is there any breach of ethical standards?

2　A colleague receives three tenders and is undertaking an evaluation of these bids. After your colleague has made a phone call to one of the bidders, you notice that they amend the prices stated in the supplier's tender. You realise that this makes their tender the lowest price, and so they are more likely to be awarded the contract. Has your colleague been ethical in their dealings with the supplier?

3　In a tendering exercise, you receive a phone call from one of the suppliers informing you that they made a mistake when pricing their bid. They had over-estimated the costs of scaffolding, and would now like to reduce their price by £22,000. You notice that this amendment makes the supplier's bid the most advantageous. Would you accept this reduction in their tendered price owing to their mistake?

4　Your organisation operates a strict tendering procedure whereby all tenders submitted have to be received by a specified date and time. Tenders for one job should be received today, by 11.00 a.m. However, you receive a phone call at 10.45 from one of the tenderers saying that their bid is not ready, and they would like another two days to prepare their tender. You need to decide whether it would be unethical to grant this extension of time.

Feedback on page 206

Revision question for study session 12

1　Draw a diagram illustrating the 11 stages of the purchasing cycle in order.
2　Describe the request for quotation (RFQ) process.
3　Describe the vendor rating process including giving a summary of the criteria you might use.

Feedback on page 207

Revision question for study session 13

1　Identify five sources of information on potential suppliers.
2　Explain in detail why it is advisable to carry out supplier appraisal before awarding contracts.
3　Describe the kind of information you should find out about potential suppliers when carrying out supplier appraisal.

Feedback on page 208

Revision question for study session 14

1　List five pieces of information that a purchase order should contain.

2 Write a report to your subordinates indicating how the vendor rating process should be carried out.
3 List five pieces of information that an RFQ should contain.
4 Suggest five aspects of environmental capability that buyers should be concerned about in relation to suppliers.

Feedback on page 209

Revision question for study session 15

Explain the nature of five financial ratios including their purpose and how they might be calculated.

Feedback on page 210

Revision question for study session 16

1 Briefly explain the differences between civil law and criminal law.
2 Describe two types of organisation that are subject to EU procurement directives.
3 Identify five types of law court operating in England.
4 Identify and briefly explain three statutes that affect purchasing and supply.

Feedback on page 210

Revision question for study session 17

Identify and describe five essential elements of a contract.

Feedback on page 211

Revision question for study session 18

1 Write a report to your line manager indicating the basic nature and role of conditions and warranties.
2 Explain the differences between express and implied terms of a contract.
3 Draft a contractual clause that you would insert into a contract to cover *force majeure*.

Feedback on page 212

Revision question for study session 19

1 Draft a report to colleagues outlining the legal principle of privity of contract. Use examples where necessary.
2 Describe 'collateral' contracts.
3 Explain the provisions of the Contracts, Rights of Third Parties Act 1999.

Feedback on page 212

Revision question for study session 20

Your organisation has recently been experiencing difficulties because suppliers have, on numerous occasions, either not delivered the item you have ordered or, if they have delivered, the item is found not to be working properly. Your managing director has suggested that 'delinquent' suppliers should be sued without question. You, however, are not so sure that this is the best way to proceed and you decide to investigate methods of resolving disputes between your company and suppliers.

Prepare a report, therefore, outlining your findings in the above area. Your report should focus on litigation, arbitration, adjudication and negotiation as means of dispute resolution and should include advantages of each method and any drawbacks. You should also, as part of your report, try to recommend which dispute resolution to use.

Feedback on page 213

Feedback on revision question

Feedback on revision question for study session 1

The main thing to be aware of with a question such as this is that roughly equal marks are given to each section. Then you need to think about the basic role of purchasing in the three types of organisation mentioned. The kind of things you should mention are as follows:

1   Manufacturing: the main role of purchasing is to buy the materials and components required to keep the production line operating. This involves the frequent resupply of items, often on a JIT basis. Purchasing also buys equipment and machinery to support the production process as well as spares and consumables.
2   Service providers: here the main role of purchasing is to buy equipment, materials and so on that might be required to support the service provision such as food and drink for an outside caterer. Purchasing might also buy specialist services to support the main service provided by the organisation.
3   Not-for-profit organisations: here the two main purchases are materials needed to maintain the fabric of buildings, exhibits and so on in, for example, churches and museums, and gifts and souvenirs for organisations such as these as well as for charities. The main focus is to ensure good value so that as much money as possible from donations is available for the cause represented by the organisation.

In answering such questions, you need to explain the issues you raise as much as possible and use examples.

Feedback on revision question for study session 2

To answer this kind of question you need to write an essay.

The main area of focus is to explain that quality control is basically about monitoring the quality of incoming material after it has been produced, identifying faults if there are any and rectifying the problems. The role of buyers in this process is to inform suppliers of problems and that of suppliers is to rectify them. Buyers might also look to purchase the items from elsewhere if the original supplier is not willing or able to rectify the problem identified.

In quality assurance the main focus is to try to prevent problems from occurring in the first place. The role of buyers here is to ensure that they have quality capable suppliers by carrying out supplier evaluation before awarding contracts to suppliers and carrying out vendor rating to monitor suppliers' performance after contract award has taken place. The role of suppliers is to ensure that they have robust quality systems and where possible, make suggestions that might improve the achievement of good quality.

Feedback on revision question for study session 3

The first thing to do here is to focus on the command word: 'explain'. This means that you need to give a detailed explanation of the issues being questioned rather than just a brief mention. This might seem obvious but many students do not explain things in anything like enough detail.

1   EOQ attempts to optimise the cost of acquisition of items by striking a balance between ordering costs and stockholding costs. You should explain that the process of placing orders has a cost to the organisation and that, if you place small orders frequently to reduce stockholding, the cost of ordering taken over the year increases. Conversely, if you hold large quantities of stock, the various costs of stockholding – you should explain these: capital tied up, rent/rates staff and so on – will increase.

2   The fixed order point method of re-ordering involves having a maximum stock level usually based on use over a period and a minimum stock level usually based on the item's lead time. A re-order level is then calculated, based on the item's lead time and its reliability (the lead time not the item itself!). When stock, which is reduced over time by use, reaches the re-order level, an order is placed with the supplier for replacements.

Feedback on revision question for study session 4

In this kind of question, full explanation is required for (1), whereas mere mention (listing) is required for (2).

1   The decision about the type of transport to be used depends on issues such as where the item is coming from (for example, heavy or large items coming from overseas must make a large part of their journey by sea). Other considerations are the nature of the goods: for instance, many 'dangerous' items cannot go by air; and the speed with which goods are needed. All such instances should be explained with examples where possible.

2   Hazards can include: movement of the transport type (for example, the motion of the sea), extreme heat, extreme cold, wet/humid conditions and extremely dry conditions. These factors might not be important for many items but for many others they will. Detailed explanation in this type of question will not gain you extra marks.

Feedback on revision question for study session 5

1   On-time delivery is important to purchasers in every possible purchasing situation. You could sum this point up by saying that without on-time delivery of supplies, no organisation would be able to perform its operations, be they production or service related.

2   There are many concepts of lead time, which are demonstrated by figure 5.1. Total, or 'true', lead time may be described as the time between the need being recognised and its being completely satisfied. This time includes the time taken to alert the purchasing department to the need, the sourcing process, awarding contracts (assuming the item has not been purchased previously), the supplier's manufacturing time (assuming the purchase is a tangible item rather than a service), delivery time, and the time taken between receiving the goods, checking them and making them available to the user department. Using figure 5.1 as an example is perfectly acceptable providing you get it right!

3   Expediting is important because it is useful to monitor the supplier's performance in producing the item purchased and ensuring its timely delivery. This should take place for every purchase, particularly those with long lead times and those that are of particular importance to the purchasing organisation. Measuring a supplier's performance over time is important to give the buyer information as to which suppliers are 'good' suppliers in terms of delivery and quality. Sometimes the phrase 'quality of service' is used to combine these considerations.

Feedback on revision question for study session 6

In this question you have a range of different tasks for which you have to provide good answers. In the first part you need to write an essay explaining total acquisition costs in some depth. In the second part you have a task that is fairly rare in purchasing exams, that of drawing a diagram. In the third part you have to give five *brief* explanations of pricing policies (one or two sentences should suffice).

1   Here you need to explain total acquisition cost, emphasising that it is much more than the purchase price and includes such things as the cost of ordering and the cost of delivery as well as the cost of any additional work that might need to be done after delivery.

2   The diagram should be similar to the one you have seen in this study session.

3   Here you need to select any five pricing policies such as 'skimming', short-term profit maximisation, market entry pricing, loss leadership, product range pricing, 'peak' and 'off-peak' pricing, and so on.

Feedback on revision question for study session 7

This question contains several short parts. Only part (3) requires anything like a full explanation approaching an essay. The other parts only require brief identification (in other words little more than brief statements) of points. You should remember that, if you spend too much time on questions such as part (1), you will not gain any more marks and you will be wasting time that could be better spent gaining marks elsewhere.

1   You should state that a specification is a means of accurately describing something of a technical nature.

2   Two aspects of specifications that might have legal implications might be whether an item supplied against a performance specification is fit for the purpose intended or if a specification has health and safety implications.

3   This part requires a reasonably full explanation and should focus on the commercial implications of specifications so that you should describe such issues as whether it specifies commercially available items or whether the item specified is 'standard' as opposed to 'special'. The ability of buyers to bring in suppliers at the design stage (EBI/ESI) should be included here.

4   Tolerances are ways of describing acceptable boundaries around a requested dimension within which actual dimensions are acceptable.

5   You should state such things as the fact that specifications must be clear and unambiguous, should not have tolerances that are too 'tight', must be easily communicated and should allow room for technical input from the supplier.

Feedback on revision question for study session 8

The important thing here is to take a practical approach, particularly to the second part: the description of situations. Use examples from your own experience if you wish. Remember in general that examples of issues from your own experience are perfectly acceptable ways of answering exam questions.

You have a range of specification types to choose from:

- Drawings, which are used to describe technical, usually engineering, items.
- Brand names, which are used where a specific product is required.
- Standards, which widen the potential supply market.
- Performance specifications, which encourage supplier contribution to the specification.
- Material and method of manufacture, which are used when the buyer wants to exert a high degree of control over the way in which the supplier produces the required item.
- Chemical and physical specifications, which are used, in the main, for raw materials.

Feedback on revision question for study session 9

1   Typical problems might be that the supplier will look after its own interests at the expense of the buyer's and that involving a supplier in the design of something purchased might 'tie' the buyer to that supplier, whose performance might start to deteriorate after time. Another problem would be if the item designed with a supplier's collaboration fails, who pays? There is a selection of three potential problems here but if you can think of others, include them, although always remember that, in a question such as this one, only *two* problems are required.

2   Typical problems might include:
- Over-specification although you might find this difficult to identify unless you have considerable experience. This often occurs because the user, quite understandably, wants to ensure that the item purchased does the job for which it is required successfully.
- Specification that effectively 'ties' you to one supplier, giving you little scope to source the market to obtain the best deal.

- Specifying something that is very difficult to find in the market.
- Specification of a 'special' when there are standard items available that will probably perform the required function adequately.

3 Typical issues that buyers need to be aware of include such possibilities as:

- Users writing specifications around a particular item, thus preventing competition.
- The specification by users of custom-built items when acceptable standard items are available.
- Users specifying something that does not exist in the market place, or which will be difficult to source.
- Users over-specifying, for example using unnecessarily tight tolerances, or extra functions that are not necessary.
- Sometimes many very similar specifications exist but with each one being slightly different from the others. In this situation buyers should try to encourage users to standardise.
- Occasionally suppliers' representatives will go directly to users and convince them that their product is the one that should be used, leading to specifications being written around the supplier's product specification. This ignores the possibility that other suppliers might offer something just as good but at a lower price. Buyers having knowledge of specifications would be aware of such situations and could try to prevent them.

You only need to describe any four of these. The information might seem somewhat 'hard' on users but you should remember that commercial issues are not part of users' remit.

4 Given the nature of the question you only need to state contributions briefly. They would include:

- Use of supplier's expertise to give better technical features at the best price.
- Early identification of potential cost savings.
- Suggestions from the supplier of different/better ways of achieving product/service goals.
- For service provision it is highly likely that service providers would be brought in to advise on the requirements that the service would address.
- Suggestions regarding delivery packaging.
- Suggestions regarding transport.

Any five of these would suffice.

5 Buyers could make contributions in:

- Language, and the different meaning of certain terms in different languages.
- National standards, regulations and codes of practice, some of which may be required by law.
- Different legal systems that might be encountered when buying from overseas, which might impact on specifications.

Any two of these would suffice.

Feedback on revision question for study session 10

1 You should briefly explain that a budget is a forecast of expenditure that is used as a *guide* to expenditure over a forthcoming period. It is

not intended to be a finite amount of money which, when spent, is 'all gone'.

2   Your answer should include any five of the following points.

- **Reliability**: consistency of performance and dependability meaning that the firm performs the service right first time and honours its promises.
- **Responsiveness**: the willingness and readiness of employees to provide the service including timeliness.
- **Competence**: the required skills and knowledge to perform the service.
- **Access**: approachability and ease of contact.
- **Courtesy**: politeness, respect, consideration and friendliness of contact personnel including receptionists and telephonists.
- **Communication**: keeping customers informed in a language they can understand, which may mean adjusting it for different customers.
- **Credibility**: trustworthiness, honesty and believability: having the customer's best interests at heart.
- **Security**: freedom from danger, risk or doubt.
- **Understanding**: making the effort to understand the customer's needs.
- **Tangibles**: physical evidence of the service.

3   As with the previous question, any five of the following list of 'characteristics' would suffice. Any other reasonable point apart from those on the list would also gain marks.

- **Performance**: primary operating characteristics.
- **Features**: the 'bells and whistles': extras provided that are not essential to the product's performance.
- **Conformance**: the degree to which the design matches known or agreed standards.
- **Reliability**: the likelihood of failure in a given time period.
- **Durability**: the useful life of the product.
- **Serviceability**: speed, ease and cost of maintenance.
- **Aesthetics**: the look, feel, sound, taste and smell of a product.
- **Perceived quality**: brand image and reputation.

4   Your answer should explain that 'standard' items are readily available for purchase whereas 'specials' are made to order, often to the design of the purchaser. 'Special' items usually cost more than 'standard' items.

Feedback on revision question for study session 11

All of these situations are intended to provide a challenge and so, in some cases, there is no *definite* right or wrong answer and credit would be given for the argument you made. Marks would be given for argument containing something like the following detail:

1   There is not *necessarily* a breach of ethical standards because there is no proof that anyone – your manager or their relative – has gained from the arrangement but it is, nonetheless, suspicious. Because of this, it is behaviour that would not be recommended. At the very least, your manager should have made the connection with the supplier clear.

2 It would appear that the colleague has not been ethical. Again, it is a little difficult because you do not know what was said in the telephone conversation. However, it would appear that the likelihood is that the colleague told the supplier what price it needed to beat to be the lowest bidder: very unethical if it happened because, apart from anything else, it makes a mockery of the competitive tendering process.

3 There is nothing here to suggest that anything necessarily untoward is happening. Mistakes can be made and there is no suggestion that anyone is making any personal gain from allowing the supplier to re-tender. If you wanted to be 'squeaky clean' and remove any doubt, you could always cover yourself by giving all of the other bidders the opportunity to re-tender if they wished.

4 Here again, there is no direct suggestion that anyone is likely to gain out of this arrangement. The problem is, however, that it might appear that way and appearances can be as harmful as the actuality. Realistically, to preserve your reputation for ethical conduct at all times, the only thing you can do is either to reject the supplier's request or accept it and give all of the other tenderers the same opportunity to extend their time to prepare their tenders. However, given the late hour of the request, other tenderers might not be too happy about an extension granted on any grounds.

Feedback on revision question for study session 12

1 Your diagram should look something like figure 21.1:

Figure 21.1

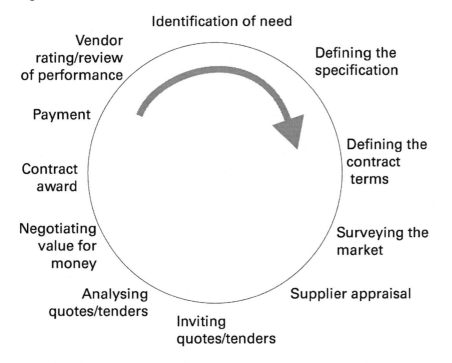

2 The RFQ process involves the buyer putting the specification(s) of the required item with other important information for potential suppliers, such as quantity required, delivery time required, terms and conditions, information about the buyer's company, delivery address(es) and so on.

They send this out to prospective suppliers to enable them to submit a quote if they are able to supply the goods or service.

3   Vendor rating is a process of monitoring/measuring a supplier's performance *post contract*. It involves measuring such aspects of suppliers' performance as quality (which might be measured by counting the percentage of rejects, either at goods inward or on the production line) and service (which might be counting the number of late deliveries). Some buyers put other performance measures such as ability to respond to questions/complaints, promptness of invoice provision and so on into their vendor rating programmes.

Feedback on revision question for study session 13

1   Five sources of information on potential suppliers might be:
   - purchase department records
   - internet (used increasingly these days)
   - suppliers' representatives
   - trade exhibitions
   - other personnel
   - trade associations or organisations such as CIPS.

Any five (or any other not on this list) would suffice. All you need to do on a question of this nature is to state the sources: no detailed explanation is necessary.

2   Your answer, which should be in essay form, should be based on the fact that potential suppliers are unknown quantities; they may be good suppliers, they may not. The purpose of supplier appraisal, therefore, is to ascertain as much as possible that the potential supplier will prove to be a good supplier in all aspects of supplier performance: quality, service, reliability and ease of communication. You might also try to ascertain the supplier's level of flexibility in terms of dealing with queries and so on.

3   Your answer here could be in essay form or 'bullet points' although, if you choose the latter format, you should give a brief explanation of each point. The kind of information you should try to find out during supplier appraisal would be:
   - What quality systems do they have including are they accredited to, for example, ISO 9000?
   - Is their production properly controlled in terms of flow down the production line or does it appear to be haphazard?
   - How capable is the supplier's management? This will dictate, to a great extent, how good a supplier the company proves to be and may be judged by aspects such as general housekeeping, staff morale and the presence, or otherwise, of systems.
   - What is the supplier's financial position? This may be judged from analysis of balance sheets, profit and loss accounts or by obtaining Dun & Bradstreet reports.
   - What is the supplier's commercial ability: how experienced are they in providing the kind of product or service that you would be purchasing from them? What systems and procedures do they

have for such things as invoicing? Do they have full electronic communication capability?

- What technical expertise do they have? Would they be able to be innovative or to contribute to ESI?

Feedback on revision question for study session 14

1   There is much information that a purchase order should contain. Typically, this might be:
    - specification of items or service required
    - quantity or quantities for repeat deliveries
    - delivery location(s)
    - required delivery time
    - price (having been agreed with the seller)
    - date
    - order number
    - internal reference.

    Any five of these points (or any other relevant point) would earn a mark and again, in a question such as this, you only need to state the point rather than explain it.

2   This answer should be in report format although the marks are awarded for correct information rather than format. The vendor rating process involves measuring a supplier's actual performance *after a contract has been awarded*. This measurement can then be repeated over time to build up a picture of whether the supplier is a 'good' supplier. The process usually involves measuring such aspects of performance as quality, which can be measured by calculating the percentage of rejects, either at goods inward or on the production line. Service quality can be measured by measuring the percentage of late deliveries, and the supplier's price capability can be measured by comparing the price actually paid to the supplier with prices quoted by other suppliers at the tendering stage. Some buyers try to measure other aspects of performance such as the supplier's ability to deal with complaints, but these are more subjective issues that can really only be measured by asking other personnel for their views.

3   This question is similar in nature to (1): all you need to do is mention five pieces of information. These might be any five from:
    - Date.
    - Purchaser's name and contact details.
    - Specification of the item(s) required.
    - Quantity or quantities for repeat deliveries.
    - Delivery location(s).
    - Buyer's signature.
    - Space for the supplier to enter the price and other details.
    - A formal request to the supplier stating something such as 'please provide your best terms …'. This is done so that the supplier is clear that the document is not a purchase order.

    Credit would be given for any other reasonable point.

4   Once again, this is a similar type of question to (1) and (3), in that you only need to state five points. These might be:
    - The supplier buying raw material from sustainable resources.
    - The supplier not polluting the environment.

- How the supplier disposes of waste.
- Whether the supplier's product is dangerous or environmentally threatening when in use.
- To what extent the supplier recycles material.

Again, any other reasonable point would gain credit.

Feedback on revision question for study session 15

Your answer should focus on any five of the following ratios:

Profitability:

Profit margin = (Profit before interest and tax ÷ sales revenue (turnover)) × 100

Profitability = (Profit before interest and tax ÷ total assets) × 100

Return on capital employed = (Profit before interest and tax ÷ capital employed) × 100

(Capital employed = shareholders' funds + long-term loans)

Liquidity:

Current ratio = Current assets ÷ current liabilities

Acid or quick ratio = Current assets less stock ÷ current liabilities

Stock turnover = Cost of sales ÷ stock

Credit period = (Debtors ÷ sales revenue) × 365 days

Gearing = Long-term loans ÷ shareholders' funds

Financial markets:

Return on shareholders' funds = (Profit after interest and tax ÷ shareholders' funds) × 100

You should show the methods of calculation, as indicated above, and provide an explanation of what each ratio that you select tries to show about a supplier's performance. An example would be that the profitability ratio shows what kind of profit the supplier is making; too high and it suggests that the supplier is charging prices that are too high, too low and it suggests that the supplier's future is uncertain.

Feedback on revision question for study session 16

1   This is another essay-type question. You should explain that criminal law involves alleged criminals, that is: people who have committed murder, robbery and so on, being prosecuted by the police (through the Crown Prosecution Service). If they are found guilty they are punished

by imprisonment, fine or community service (or a combination of these). On the other hand, civil law involves someone who believes that they have been wronged in some way by someone else taking that person to court to claim damages. If the action is successful the defendant has to pay the plaintiff (the person who brought the action) damages or compensate them in some other way. Criminal law is about punishment whereas civil law is about compensation.

2 Here a brief description of the two types of organisation is required. They are: public sector organisations such as local authorities and NHS trusts, and private companies that provide public services or utilities such as water companies. Technically, these private companies must be operating in regulated industries. This usually means that they are, in effect, monopolies.

3 Again, this question only requires brief statements. The types of court are:
   • Magistrates' court
   • Small claims court
   • Crown Court
   • High Court
   • Court of Appeal.

4 Here you need to give any three of the following with a brief explanation of what they cover and try to achieve:
   • Sale of Goods Act 1979. This confers certain rights to the buyer and obligations on the seller, such as the fact that the goods must be fit for the purpose specified, for contracts involving the *sale* of *goods* (that is, not for services or 'barter' transactions).
   • Supply of Goods and Services Act 1982. This, in essence, gives the same conditions as in the 1979 Act to contracts involving services and/or barter or exchange.
   • Sale and Supply of Goods Act 1994. This modifies the 1979 Act in some important areas, the main one being that 'merchantable quality' becomes 'satisfactory quality' and the Act provides guidelines as to what constitutes 'satisfactory quality'.
   • Unfair Contract Terms Act 1977. This stipulates that neither party to a contract should include terms that could be construed as being unfair to the other party. Whereas the main function of the other Acts is to protect the buyer, this one protects both parties, as necessary.

Feedback on revision question for study session 17

Here you need to take any five of the following and give a brief explanation of their function:

• Offer: this can be an offer to buy or an offer to sell. It can be made to an individual or to the world at large.
• Acceptance: this is a response to the offer that must agree in all respects with the offer. You could state that a response that accepts much of the offer but that does not agree with part of it is a counter offer rather than acceptance.
• Intention to create legal relations: both parties to the contract must demonstrate that they intend that the agreement should be legally

binding. In the commercial world this is normally achieved by having documents labelled 'purchase order' or 'acknowledgement'.

- Capacity: this is legal capacity. Everyone over the age of 18 has capacity to enter into contracts for themselves, but the concept of capacity of an organisation's employees is more complicated, depending on the perception of the other party.
- Legality: a contract cannot be for an illegal purpose.
- Consideration: this is the price paid by the buyer in return for goods or services provided by the seller. In commercial purchasing, consideration is usually the money paid, but it does not need to be money: exchange can count but consideration must be something of value.

Feedback on revision question for study session 18

1   You should explain that the 'small print' of a contract is known collectively as 'terms' and that these are the 'rules' by which the parties intend to play the purchasing 'game'. In other words, they limit and set parameters on certain aspects of the agreement. Terms are divided into 'conditions' and 'warranties'. Conditions are terms that go to the heart of the contract (that is, they are fundamental to the contract's satisfactory performance) and warranties are minor terms that are more peripheral to the contract's performance. If a condition is breached, the successful plaintiff can be awarded damages, repudiation (in effect, terminating the contract) might be allowed, as would rescission (returning to a state of affairs that existed before the contract was made). An award of 'specific performance' might be made against the defendant, meaning that the defendant would be required by the court to complete the contract under its terms. A combination of some of these, for example damages and specific performance, might be made. If a warranty is breached, the plaintiff can only receive damages.

2   Express terms are ones that are specifically stated in the contract, for example that the contract must be completed by a certain date. Implied terms are ones that are not necessarily discussed but that both parties and indeed the world at large would take for granted. An example here would be that if you buy a car, you do not need to state that you want it for travelling in; it is widely accepted that this is why people buy cars. Some terms can be implied by legislation, for example the Sale of Goods Act 1979 provides an implied term that the seller has the right to sell the goods.

3   This question allows some creativity. *Force majeure* means circumstances outside one of the party's control preventing them from performing their side of the contract. The actual wording of your clause is not important as long as the meaning is clear. Typical wording might be that 'we will not be liable for the non-performance of the contract due to circumstances outside our control'. You might want to add examples such as fire, flood, breakdown of outside transport and so on.

Feedback on revision question for study session 19

1   Again, this answer should be in report form although marks are awarded, in the main, for content rather than format. Privity of contract

means that only the parties that made the contract can be bound by its provisions and that third parties cannot. An example might be where someone buys a gift for someone else and the gift proves to be faulty. The recipient of the gift, not being party to the contract, would not be able to sue the seller because they do not have a contract with the seller.

2 A collateral contract, essentially, is where a third party, for example a named subcontractor, is included in the contract. This modifies the principle of privity of contract.

3 Again, this piece of legislation modifies the principle of privity of contract. It lays down that a third party may enforce rights under a contract where:

   - The party is expressly given the right to do so under the contract.
   - The contract purports to confer a benefit on that party.
   - The parties to a contract have not made it clear that they intended to exclude that third party from having the right to enforce it.

Typically, third parties in this context would be agents or subcontractors.

Feedback on revision question for study session 20

Here, you should take each of the possible means of dispute resolution mentioned in the question and describe it, explaining advantages and disadvantages. The means of dispute resolution are as follows:

- Negotiation: the cheapest and easiest method, also the quickest. It involves both parties coming together to discuss their differences and reach a conclusion that will satisfy both parties. Its drawback is that no resolution might be reached.
- Adjudication: resolution by expert determination. A third party is nominated who will hear both parties' side of the story and will determine an outcome. If both parties agree, the outcome can be considered legally binding. It is cheaper and quicker than arbitration and litigation but there is the danger that the adjudicator might show bias.
- Arbitration: this, again, involves both parties appointing a third party to decide upon their dispute. It is more formal and therefore more expensive than adjudication and, if both parties agree, the outcome can be legally binding. It is much used to resolve international disputes.
- Litigation: this is the court process where the aggrieved party sues the other for damages or some other form of recompense. It is expensive and time-consuming compared to other dispute resolution methods but has the advantage of being legally binding although there is an appeal process if the party that 'loses' is not happy with the verdict.

Recommendation is difficult because each dispute is different with different circumstances, but generally negotiation is the preferred option at least to begin with. Certainly, it should be tried before any of the other resolution method is invoked.

References and bibliography

This section contains a complete A-Z listing of all publications, materials or websites referred to in this course book. Books, articles and research are listed under the first author's (or in some cases the editor's) surname. Where no author name has been given, the publication is listed under the name of the organisation that published it. Websites are listed under the name of the organisation providing the website.

Baily, P, D Farmer, D Jessop and D Jones (2004) *Purchasing Principles and Management*, 9th edition. FT Prentice Hall

Carter, R and S Kirby (forthcoming 2006) *Practical Procurement*, Cambridge Academic

CIPS (Chartered Institute of Purchasing & Supply): http://www.cips.org

Compare Store Prices: http://www.comparestoreprices.co.uk

Griffiths, M and I Griffiths (2002) *Law for Purchasing & Supply*, 3rd edition. FT Prentice Hall

Logismarket: http://www.logismarket.com

Lysons, K and B Farrington (2006) *Purchasing and Supply Chain Management*, 7th edition. FT Prentice Hall

Wyborn, J (2000) *One Stop Contracts*, 2nd edition. ICSA

Index

absolute capacity, 171
acceptance
    contracts, 166, 174, 175
accounting, 129, 135, 147
accreditation, 128
acid ratio, 150
acknowledgements, 139, 179
acquisition costs, 27, 58
adjudication, 191
advice notes, 139
agreements, 167
air transport, 38
appraising suppliers, 125, 145
approved bodies, 128
approved supplier lists, 134
arbitration, 191
assembly manufacturing, 2, 4
assignment clauses, 179
balance sheets, 147
battle of the forms, 175
bespoke specifications, 98
bids, 171
blueprints, 79
brand names, 78, 82
British Standards Institution (BSI),
    84
budgets, 100
buffer stocks, 29
buyers
    specification issues, 72, 89
canals
    transport, 39
capability
    supplier verification, 145
    surveys, 134
capacity
    contracts, 168
capital items, 4
case law, 158
CEN see European Committee for
    Standardization
chancery, 160
charities, 2, 8
chemical specifications, 79

civil courts, 160
civil law, 159, 161
clauses in contracts, 177, 179
collateral contracts, 185, 187
commercial capabilities, 135
common law, 158
company standard contracts, 169
composition specifications, 82
computer-controlled processes, 4
conditions in contracts, 173
conflict of interest, 108
conformance to specification, 14
consensus ad idem, 167
consideration in contracts, 168
contracts
    dispute resolution, 189
    formation, 165, 184
    management, 100
    privity of contract, 183
    terms and conditions, 173
    third party rights, 185
contribution pricing, 62
control, 129
Control of Substances Hazardous to
    Health (COSHH), 109
corporate social responsibility
    (CSR), 108
COSHH see Control of Substances
    Hazardous to Health
costs, 15, 59, 100
counter offers, 167, 174, 175
County Court, 160
Court of Appeal, 160
courts, 159, 192
credit period, 150
criminal law, 159, 161
Crown Court, 160
CSR see corporate social
    responsibility
current ratio, 150
damage clauses, 177, 179
delivered duty paid (DDP), 46

delivery issues
    lead times, 48
    right place, 35
    right time, 47
    specifications, 73
    terms and conditions of
        contract, 179
    transport types, 37
demand factors, 24
Directives, 161
directories, 126
dispute resolution, 189
documentation requirements, 133
drawings, 79
driving the specification, 72
early buyer involvement (EBI), 89,
    91
early supplier involvement (ESI),
    89, 93, 153
economic order quantity (EOQ),
    27
electronic point of sale (EPOS), 11
engineering drawings, 81
English legal system, 157
enterprise resource planning (ERP),
    94
environmental capabilities, 135
EOQ see economic order quantity
EPOS see electronic point of sale
ERP see Enterprise Resource
    Planning
ESI see early supplier involvement
ethics, 108
European Committee for
    Standardization (CEN), 84
European law, 161
European Union (EU), 84, 161
evaluating supply sources, 125
exceptions to privity of contract,
    185
exhibitions, 126
expediting delivery times, 51
expenditure budgets, 100
express terms, 176
external influences to specifications,
    107
external lead times, 49
ex-works (EXW) deliveries, 46
factoring, 3, 82
failure mode and effects analysis
    (FMEA), 18

family division
    High Court, 160
fast moving consumer goods
    (FMCG), 6, 82
finance
    appraisals, 147
    financial markets, 151
    ratio analysis, 150
    sourcing documentation, 135
    stability
fitness for purpose, 14, 69
FMCG see fast moving consumer
    goods
FMEA see failure mode and effects
    analysis
following up references, 146
force majeure, 177
functional specifications, 82
gearing, 150
goods received notes (GRN), 139
gross profit, 149
High Court, 160
identification of needs, 116
identifying supply sources, 125
implied terms, 176
Incoterms , 41
industry standards, 84
information issues
    potential suppliers, 126
    specifications, 97
inland waterways, 39
innovation of suppliers, 153
inspections
    contracts, 179
insurance stocks, 29
intention to be legally bound, 167
interest conflicts, 108
internal influences to specifications,
    107
internal lead times, 49
International Standards
    Organization (ISO), 84
international transport
    documentation, 41
internet, 126
invitations to bid, 136
invitations to treat, 166
invoices, 139
ISO see International Standards
    Organization
journals, 126
judiciary, 157

just-in-time (JIT) process, 4
kite-marks, 109
last document rule, 175
law, 157, 168 *see also* legal
    regulations and frameworks
    See also;z, 168
lead times, 48
legal regulations and frameworks,
    157
    contract formation, 168
    specifications, 109
letters of credit, 41
liquidated damages, 177
liquidity, 150
litigation, 192
logistics operators, 52
losses, 149
loss in transit clauses, 179
loss leaders, 62
made to order specifications, 98
Magistrates Court, 160
mail, 126
maintenance repair and operational
    (MRO) items, 9
management ability, 129
managing supplier's quality, 17
manufacturing sector, 2, 3, 81
market penetration, 61
market surveying, 117
material requirements planning
    (MRP), 4
minimum order quantities (MOQ),
    25
model forms of contract, 169
monitoring performance, 121
MOQ *see* minimum order
    quantities
MRO *see* maintenance repair and
    operational
MRP *see* material requirements
    planning
national standards, 84
nature of organisation differences, 2
needs identification, 116
negotiation
    contract dispute resolution, 190
    European law, 162
    purchasing cycles, 120
non-production purchases, 4
not-for-profit organisations, 2, 8,
    82

offers
    contracts, 166, 174
Official Journal of the European
    Union (OJEU), 161
off-peak pricing, 62
OJEU *see* Official Journal of the
    European Union
on-time deliveries, 47
open procedure in European law,
    162
open tendering, 123
organisational policies, 107
organisations and purchasing
    objectives, 1
packaging considerations, 43
packing, 179
packing notes, 139
parliament, 157
passage of risk, 178
passing of property, 177, 179
payment clauses, 179
payment methods, 140
payment practices, 110
peak pricing
performance reviews, 121
performance specifications, 78, 82
physical specifications, 79
placement issues, 35
pricing, 57, 110
private sector service organisations,
    5
privity of contract, 183
    concept, 184
    exceptions, 185
processing organisations, 3
procurement directives, 161
product complexity, 4
production capabilities, 134
production control, 129
production facilities, 128
product quality, 99
product specifications, 69
profit, 62, 149
profitability ratios, 150
property specifications, 79
public sector service organisations ,
    5
published standards, 84, 109
purchase orders, 139, 170
purchase to pay process, 138
purchasing cycles, 115
purchasing documentation, 133

purchasing objectives in different
    organisations, 1
QA *see* quality assurance
QC *see* quality control
quality
    achievement, 13
    costs involved in getting it
        wrong, 15
    fitness for purpose, 14
    management, 18
    purchasing objectives, 4
    specifications, 99
    standards, 109
quality assurance (QA), 17
quality control (QC), 17
quantity issues, 23
Queen's Bench division, 160
questionnaires, 127
quick ratio, 150
quotations, 119, 136, 171
rail transport, 38
ratio analysis, 150
reference follow up, 146
registers, 126
rejection clauses, 179
religious establishments, 2, 8
reorder points, 29
representatives, 126
reputation
    suppliers, 128
requests for quotation (RFQ), 119,
    136
resolving contractual disputes, 189
restricted procedure, 162
re-supply needs, 4
retailing organisations, 2, 6, 82
retention of title, 179
reviewing performance, 121
RFQ *see* requests for quotation
right price, 57
    paying, 58
    suppliers pricing factors, 59
risks in contracts, 178
road transport, 38
safety stocks, 29
Sale of Goods Act 1979, 163
samples, 79, 82
scheduling systems, 30
sea transport, 39
sellers and specification
    development, 89
service delivery issues, 71

service level agreements, 71
service organisations, 2, 5
service provision, 4
service specifications, 70, 82
shareholders funds, 151
short-term profit maximisation, 61
skimming, 61
social responsibility, 108
sourcing documentation, 133
special contract terms, 177
specifications
    buyer contribution, 89
    conformance, 14
    definitions, 68
    external influences, 107
    importance, 69
    information requirements, 97
    internal influences, 107
    legal factors, 72
    purchasing cycles, 116
    purpose of, 67
    service, 70
    supplier contribution, 89
    types, 77
standard contractual forms, 169
standardisation, 85
standards
    features, 84
    information requirements', 98
    sources, 84
    specification influences, 109
    specification types, 79, 84
statute law, 158
stock replenishment, 29
sub-assemblies, 4
subcontracting, 179, 184
suppliers
    appraisals, 118, 145
    capability verification, 145
    delivery performance, 52
    evaluation, 125
    financial appraisals, 147
    information issues, 126
    performance, 145
    purchasing cycles, 118
    reference follow up, 146
    right price issues, 59
    supplier catalogues, 126
Supply of Goods and Services Act
    1982, 163
surveying the market, 117
technical ability, 128

technical specifications, 80, 81, 99
templates
    contracts, 169
tendering, 119, 136, 171
terms and conditions
    contracts, 173
    definition, 174
    role, 174
testing
    contracts, 179
third party rights, 185
time issues, 100, 179
title
    retention of, 177, 179
tolerances, 68
total acquisition costs, 137
total lead times, 49
trade exhibitions, 126
trade journals, 126
trade registers
transport types, 37
Unfair Contract Terms Act 1977,
    163
value for money, 101, 137
variations in contracts, 179
vendor ratings, 138
visiting potential suppliers, 127
volume capability verification, 152
warranties, 176
wholesaling organisations, 3, 82
zero defects, 18